AMERICAN ◆ CLASSICS

LINCOLN
1945–1995

Gregory Von Dare

Motorbooks International
Publishers & Wholesalers ®

First published in 1995 by Motorbooks International Publishers & Wholesalers, PO Box 2, 729 Prospect Avenue, Osceola, WI 54020 USA

Motorbooks International books are also available at discounts in bulk quantity for industrial or sales-promotional use. For details write to Special Sales Manager at the Publisher's address

Library of Congress Cataloging-in-Publication Data
Von Dare, Gregory.
    Lincoln 1945-1995 / Gregory Von Dare.
       p.   cm.
    Includes index.
    1. Lincoln automobile—History.
    2. Lincoln Motor Company
(Detrooit, Mich.)—History. I. Title.
Tl215.L5V56 1995
338.7'6292222—dc20   95-12519

On the front cover: This stunning 1952 Capri convertible is owned by Carl and Mary Allen of Naples, Florida. Lincoln produced just 1,191 examples of this model, the rarest of the 1952-54 generation, and they are highly sought by collectors today.

Printed and bound in the United States of America

Contents

Chapter 1

Origins—The Lincoln Motor Car Company and Its Development Through 1945

The early days of the Lincoln car are essentially the story of two extraordinary men named Henry: Henry Leland and Henry Ford. Most automobiles are lucky to be designed by proficient engineers. Some, a Porsche or Bugatti, have the distinction of being created by automotive geniuses, but it is rare when two acknowledged masters add their gifts in the history of a single marque. Such is the legacy of Lincoln automobiles.

Founded by master machinist Henry Martyn Leland, the Lincoln car company was later acquired by Henry Ford and became the personal statement of his only son, Edsel. Leland's obsession with quality workmanship gave Lincoln a superb heritage of engineering, and Ford's giant organization gave the cars a wide dealer network and the support of deep pockets. With Edsel Ford in nominal charge of the company and E.T. Gregorie designing the cars, the Lincoln found a home in American culture and became one of the most respected domestic vehicles in the United States. Lincoln competed with Cadillac, Packard, Cord, Auburn, Duesenberg, Pierce-Arrow, and other giants. During the elegant years of the 1930s, Lincoln achieved a mechanical and stylistic excellence symbolized by the running greyhound hood ornament.

After the economic implosion of the Great Depression, the death of Edsel in 1943, and the cataclysm of World War II, Lincoln stumbled and lost direction. In truth, this simply reflected the upheavals in American society—and within the boardroom of Ford Motor Company. Over the last two decades, the Lincoln has reclaimed its heritage and solidified its position as *the*

American prestige car. Thanks to strong leadership, courage, and the application of some advanced technology, Lincoln is poised to enter a new golden age.

To fully understand the traditions, engineering, and evolution of Lincoln cars and the company that produced them between 1945 and 1995, we must look back to the founding of that company. Such a look requires a return to an era when there were no automobiles at all, when American transportation came in two flavors: horse and iron horse.

Industry in the nineteenth century had achieved some lofty goals. The technology of the day found its highest expression in the railroad steam engine. Huge and powerful, locomotives symbolized the restless spirit of the age. The United States expanded every day and soon filled its borders. In Europe, trains brought an unprecedented degree of communication and cultural exposure. Trade flourished everywhere as vast amounts of goods moved over the rails.

Steam locomotives were coarsely machined by our standards, with monstrously oversized parts. Many pieces of a locomotive—rods, links, and drive arms— now seem more on the scale of bridge building than transportation. Seen close-up, the steam engine is still an awesome machine, part technology, part force of nature. Despite their relative crudeness, the trains ran magnificently. Yet by the mid-1880s, after decades of successful rail travel, Europeans and Americans began tinkering with a different notion of transportation.

Personal transportation would bypass crowded, centralized train stations and give travelers the mobility

EVOLUTION OF THE
LINCOLN MOTOR CAR
1922-1968

1922
LINCOLN 4-DOOR SEDAN

1925
BRUNN BROUGHAM

1928
SPORT PHAETON

1933
DIETRICH CONVERTIBLE SEDAN

1940
CONTINENTAL COUPE

1942
CONTINENTAL CABRIOLET

1936
ZEPHYR 4-DOOR SEDAN

1946
LINCOLN 4-DOOR SEDAN

1948
CONTINENTAL 2-DOOR

1949
COSMOPOLITAN 4-DOOR

1952
CAPRI 4-DOOR

1956
PREMIER 2-DOOR HARDTOP

1961
CONTINENTAL 4-DOOR SEDAN

1965
CONTINENTAL 4-DOOR CONVERTIBLE

1956
MARK II CONTINENTAL 2-DOOR

1968
CONTINENTAL MARK III
2-DOOR COUPE

Ford
EDUCATIONAL AFFAIRS DEPARTMENT, DEARBORN, MICHIGAN
0568-5M

The poet William Blake spoke of seeing ". . . the world in a grain of sand . . ." How much can you see in this time capsule of Lincoln's evolution? *Credit: Ford Motor Company*

and door-to-door convenience of horse-drawn carriages, but with the speed of locomotives. In Germany, Gottlieb Daimler and Karl Benz independently developed primitive self-propelled buggies that abandoned the bulk of steam engines for the higher power-to-weight ratio of the internal combustion engine. The Germans ran their motors on a petroleum distillate: "benzin"—what we call gasoline.

Thus, the automobile was born. While Karl Benz' famous three-wheeler of 1886 was slow, noisy, and prone to break down, it was still an accurate prototype of the automobiles that followed it through the turn of the century. It is into this era of haphazard machining and hand fitting that our first major figure in the Lincoln story arrives.

In the United States, a Vermonter named Henry Leland had an obsession. Like few men of his era, ex-

cepting Henry Royce in England, he was devoted to mechanical precision. Leland was a Quaker farm boy who had shown a talent for making things with his hands. When Leland's mother prevented him from enlisting in the Union Army during the Civil War, he signed on at the Springfield Armory, where he worked until the end of the war machining carbines and handguns. Leland then moved to the Colt Revolver factory in Hartford, Connecticut, for a short time. There, he was exposed to ultra precise boring machines and the new idea of interchangeable parts. Finally, he took a job at the machine tool company of Browne & Sharpe.

As a traveling representative for Browne & Sharpe's machines, Leland searched the Midwest for a town in which to settle and to open a machine shop of his own. Fate had him choose Detroit, arguably the place in America where the industrial revolution would have the

The vehicle that is often called the first modern automobile is the Benz tricycle. This illustration by Ken Dallison shows inventor Karl Benz' wife Berta and their two sons taking the first automobile trip as they motored from Mannheim to Pforzheim, a distance of some 60 miles, in August 1888. *Credit: Mercedes-Benz of North America*

greatest impact. His new firm was known as Leland, Faulconer & Norton. Most of its capital came from Robert Faulconer, with Leland contributing a meager life savings. Thanks largely to Leland's obsession with precision and quality, the business thrived.

Soon, Leland brought his oldest son Wilfred into the firm. As the 1890s progressed, the business became quite successful and was soon respected nationwide as Leland & Faulconer. Eventually, Wilfred took charge of finance, leaving Henry M. Leland, "H.M." as he was called, to supervise the shop. And so he did, with a style that combined vast practical knowledge, golden-rule ethics, and a genuine concern for the welfare of his workers.

In 1899, Ransom E. Olds moved his factory to Detroit and began manufacturing motor cars there. Olds was quickly successful, but there were complaints about his cars. His vehicles were well designed but had harsh, noisy transmissions. Olds brought a gearbox to Leland & Faulconer, which by then had an excellent reputation for precision gear grinding. He asked if they could improve it. Naturally, they did. The curved-dash "Merry Oldsmobile" carried a Leland & Faulconer transmission and was one of the best-selling, best-known cars of its day.

When a fire destroyed Olds' engine department, Ransom E. turned to Leland & Faulconer to make motors for him. In this unexpected way, Henry Leland entered the trade for which he would become famous, the automobile game.

Leland & Faulconer made 2,000 engines for Olds Motor Works, and made them so well that they produced 7/10 of a horsepower more than the identical engine made by the Dodge brothers. In those days of 3hp engines, a fraction of a horsepower was a whopping difference. Legend has it that this difference in power was pointed out to Leland at the first Detroit Automobile Show in 1901 by a brash young man named Henry Ford. It would not be the last time the Lelands and the Fords crossed paths.

Fascinated by the possibilities of the internal combustion engine, an ideal subject for precision manufacture if ever there was one, Henry Leland set out to make an engine of his own. Starting with the basic Olds design, Leland had his engineers enlarge the valves and slightly change the timing of the valve train. The new motor produced well over 6hp. Olds didn't buy it because he did not want to pay the costs of retooling for the new engine. In any case, Olds soon moved his factory to Lansing, Michigan, ending his ties with Leland & Faulconer. Having experienced the excitement and enormous challenge of the automobile business, Henry Leland was firmly set on a new path that he would follow the rest of his life.

At that time, a fledgling automobile plant in Detroit was in trouble. The Henry Ford Company had been incorporated to manufacture automobiles based on Ford's original stroke of genius, the Quadracycle. But a headstrong Henry Ford didn't see eye to eye with his investors and backers. While the factory went idle, Ford built his 999 race car, the vehicle that eventually sped him to fame. Desperate financiers brought in an established engineer to rescue their business. It was Henry M. Leland.

Now, we reach a moment of uncertainty. Historical accounts of the period differ. Some of Henry Ford's biographers say Leland was hired to whip Ford into line, to disgrace him, and to teach him a lesson. Other historians claim Ford was completely out of the business before Leland became involved. The way Ford treated the Lelands some years later suggests that he carried a grudge against the rigid New Englander and his soft-spoken son. At any rate, the Henry Ford Company was quickly reorganized as the Cadillac Motor Car Company, with Leland as chief engineer. One of his first triumphs was to take the prototype engine that he fabricated for Olds and sell it to Cadillac. Rated at 9hp, the smooth-running motor was the foundation of Cadillac's reputation. At this time, Leland was sixty years old. According to a Leland biography, the first Cadillac mo-

"The master of precision," Henry Martyn Leland, was the man who made Cadillac cars a success, then founded Lincoln after World War I. Wilfred Leland, his son, was the business and finance man. Despite tireless efforts, he could not hang onto the Lincoln Company for his family. *Credit: Ford Motor Company*

Organization—Equipment—Knowing-how
Produces the new Leland-built Motor Car

In this day of big things, what more magic words than these: 'Organization,' 'Equipment,' 'Knowing-how?'

Without them is nothing great accomplished.

With them, nothing seems impossible.

Many are the stories of vast achievement in the world mechanical; among them is a story not widely known, yet a story for whose parallel you would seek far to find.

In order to understand the possibility of that achievement, let us hark back some thirty to forty years.

Then, Henry M. Leland was a conspicuous figure, in New England's higher craftsmanship.

Some years before, he had left his boyhood home on the farm in Vermont, and gone to Worcester, Mass., where he engaged as an apprentice. He became a workman at the bench, but not for long, because he soon compelled recognition as an artisan of an uncommon kind. He showed an ability to do things—to do them differently, and to do them better than they had been done before.

He became a machinery salesman, and an unusual one, because he was more than a salesman.

He knew, too, how to install and to teach the operating of the machines he sold.

Manufacturers sought his counsel. They engaged him to re-organize their equipment and their men.

He knew how to increase production, not by oppressive, but by progressive methods. He did two more things, which to those who do not know him and his methods, may seem anomalous or impossible—yet he did them.

Besides increasing volume, he actually reduced production costs, and at the same time bettered infinitely the quality of the things produced.

He had a knack and a penchant for doing things while others were saying they could not be done. His was supreme delight to bring order out of chaos.

Many are the great establishments today which owe the foundation of their prestige and their success largely to the organizing, producing and quality-building genius of Henry M. Leland.

He is credited with a multitude of "crowning achievements," because he has made it a life principle always to do things better than they had been done before.

His generalship in organization is strikingly exemplified in that of the Lincoln Motor Co., although he maintains that Wilfred C. Leland who has been his mainstay and close associate for many years, assumed a large share of the responsibilities; and to its success he also attributes the loyal, skillful and effective co-operation of his thousands of other associates.

In the year 1890 the Lelands came from New England to Detroit, where for a number of years they engaged in the manufacture of the finer kinds of machinery and precision tools. They were among the pioneers in the making of gasoline marine and automobile engines; and after eighteen years, many of those engines are still in service—a tribute to the Leland ways of doing.

Henry M. Leland, Wilfred C. Leland and some of their Chief Associates, viewing the 6,500th Lincoln Liberty Aircraft Motor

Of these nine men, seven have been in continual relation for 12 years; five for 21 years and three for 27 years

A Duplicate of this Motor is now in the Smithsonian Institution at Washington, D. C. where it will stand for all Time, a Monument to and an Example of the world's finer Craftsmanship

Shortly after our country became involved in the world conflict, the vital need for aircraft so forcibly impressed itself upon the Lelands that they severed their many years' affiliation with the motor car industry, in order that they might undertake the production of Liberty airplane motors for the allied fighting forces. This they did in July, 1917.

With absolutely nothing in the way of plant or equipment, they received the government's first award for the building of these motors and faith in the men and their ability was the government's sole assurance.

Capital was interested, and much volunteered. The Lincoln Motor Co. was formed. Fifty-two acres of land were acquired. An adequate plant was erected and equipped in record time. A vast amount of machinery was designed, built and installed. Tools to the extent of 6,522 separate and distinct designs, aggregating 91,807 in number were made.

Thousands of America's most skilled craftsmen tendered their co-operation and their services. Many of the men, particularly the executives, were men whom the Lelands knew and who knew them, through many years' association; and they were anxious to enlist under their banner.

Never in their lives, say the Lelands, have they seen such a vast organization get into working harmony with so little delay and so little friction.

The efficiency of that organization can best be appreciated when it is realized that in seven months and three days after starting with nothing, they assembled their first motor. In ten months thereafter, and with 6,000 employees, the Lincoln Motor Co. was producing at the rate of 50 motors per day. In contrast with these Leland methods, the leading English manufacturer, with three years aircraft experience and 10,000 employees, had required a week to produce the quantity of motors which the Lincoln organization had produced in a single day.

Within eleven months from the day production of completed motors began, the Lincoln Motor Co. had established the record of producing the largest number of motors in a day, the largest number in a month and the largest total produced by any manufacturer from the beginning; and those who know the story of Liberty motor building know the rivalry for that record.

The quality of Leland-built Lincoln Liberty motors has been attested by tributes and in ways which could not be misunderstood; and, too, the Lincoln Motor Co. was able to render assistance of immeasurable value to those less favorably schooled.

Assembling and harmonizing an organization expeditiously, for doing things in a big way and doing them right, is, like everything else—no matter how difficult it may seem—a plain, simple matter of 'knowing how.'

This is simplified when the executive and his chief assistants in things mechanical, can go into the shops, and with their own hands perform practically every task and operation, from the ground work to the finished product.

Such is the skill and genius; such is the organization that is producing the new Leland-built car—the car destined to chart the future course of fine car making—the car destined to prove another 'crowning achievement'—the car destined once more to demonstrate Leland determination and Leland ability to surpass.

LINCOLN MOTOR COMPANY DETROIT, MICHIGAN

This advertisement contains an interesting review of the war work of the Lincoln Motor Company which made an unparalleled record in the production of Liberty aircraft engines.

Henry Leland (at left), his son Wilfred, and several others stand around the 6500 Liberty airplane engine built by the Lelands during World War I. The Liberty was a high-power, narrow angle V-12 engine meant for fast pursuit planes and high-flying bombers. This page was an early Lincoln automobile ad. *Credit: Ford Motor Company*

tor car was completed at the Leland & Faulconer factory on October 20, 1902.

That was a remarkable era for the automobile industry. Along with Olds, the Dodge brothers, and Cadillac, Ford started up again with new backers, Packard began manufacturing, and David Dunbar Buick went into business. Every one of those names fills an encyclopedia of automotive history. In the meantime, Cadillac cars were selling as fast as they could be made.

In April 1904, a huge fire at the Cadillac works nearly destroyed the company. Fortunately, most of the completed cars were stored across the street in a warehouse that was untouched by the fire. Shortly after the fire, the Lelands took on increased duties at Cadillac. Then, in 1905, Cadillac merged with Leland & Faulconer, and the machine shop became a part of the Cadillac works.

While there were some reversals, such as a cash crunch in 1907, Cadillac was clearly on an upswing. In

This early Peugeot represented the typical European motorcar in the "teens." It was against this kind of hand-built, hand-fitted automobile that Henry Leland sought to compete with his scheme of truly interchangeable parts.
Credit: Peugeot Automobiles

1908, Cadillac introduced the Model 30, an excellent car for the time, priced at a reasonable $1,400. This car sold in volume and propelled Cadillac into the reach of more buyers while it maintained the quality and precision for which the Lelands were famous.

By 1909, Cadillac was considered one of the best brands on the American market and had attracted the interest of William Durant, the founder of General Motors Corporation (GM). In July 1909, the Lelands and their directors sold out to GM for $4.5 million, realizing a tidy profit for all involved. After the sale, Durant met with the Lelands and asked them to stay with Cadillac as managers of the company, promising them a free hand.

Through the second decade, Cadillac did well, taking a leading part in paying off GM's debt. In 1912, Cadillac introduced the electric starter and transformed the auto industry. In 1915, Cadillac developed a V-8 engine, a first for the United States. Old Henry Leland was the champion of the V-8 engine. One story claims that he had a European V-8, most likely a DeDion-

Bouton, brought in for his engineers to study. They found it crudely made by their standards, but advanced in concept.

Suddenly, war clouds darkened Europe, and the difficulties faced by the Allies—Britain, France, and others—made headlines in the United States. Although America was not yet involved in the European war, Wilfred Leland could see the day coming. He went to William Durant with a proposal that Cadillac use a newly built factory to mass produce airplane engines, which in those days were still hand-fitted.

Durant coldly rebuffed him with the statement that GM would never do work for the government. Hearing this, old Henry Leland, the man who had seen America reeling from the Civil War, erupted. He and Wilfred resigned from GM and set themselves up as airplane engine manufacturers.

The engine they would eventually manufacture did not yet exist. Soon, however, the Lelands learned of a promising design by Jesse Vincent of Packard. It was a

These two 1920 Lincolns demonstrate that the first Lincoln cars did not have styling to match their engineering; however, they were no worse looking than many other cars of the day. Perhaps the Leland name raised unrealistic expectations. *Credit: Ford Motor Company*

Henry Ford, the original American automotive genius. One of the richest men in the world in the 1920s, Ford bought the Lincoln company at a fire sale price and put his son Edsel in charge. In a few months, the Lelands were history. *Credit: Ford Motor Company*

racing V-8 rated at about 300hp. With the assistance of E.J. Hall and other engineers, this design was adapted to aircraft requirements, and, with the Lelands' help, a prototype was constructed. Then a telegram came from General John J. Pershing in Europe saying that a 300hp V-8 was not adequate for the high-speed fighters and interceptors that were needed to defeat the speedy Fokker Eindekker and agile Triplane, or to power the high-flying bombers the Allies wanted. So the 45deg V-8 design was enlarged to V-12 configuration with an output of 400hp and christened the "Liberty" engine.

The Lelands formed the Lincoln Motor Company to produce Liberty engines, naming it after H.M.'s boyhood idol, Abraham Lincoln. The Lelands expected to produce fourteen to twenty motors a day; but when the contracts for the Liberty engines were let in Washington, the Lincoln Motor Company was asked to make seventy! After the anguish of some last-minute contract adjustments, the Lelands agreed to build 6,000 Liberty engines for the government. They raised capital and built a plant to do so.

A small factory on Holden Avenue in Detroit was hurriedly equipped to begin manufacture, and construction of a giant factory on fifty acres of land off Warren Avenue began.

In typical government fashion, the approved design of the Liberty engine was not quite adequate for the demands placed on it. Engines that were supposed to run nonstop for fifty hours blew up after ten to thirty hours. When the fault was traced to weak connecting rods, it meant retooling the forgings of both the con rods and the crankshafts, a major difficulty in the midst of wartime conditions.

With their new factory built and the first Liberty engines delivered in 1918, the Lelands were delighted with their contribution to the war effort. Yet, 1918 was the year of the Armistice, and soon the Great War was over. The need for Liberty engines all but vanished.

While Henry Leland entered into the production of Liberty engines out of genuine patriotism, and while he and Wilfred negotiated a contract with the government that was standard, in years to come the US gov-

Edsel Ford was the ideal person to run the new Lincoln company. He liked big, elegant cars, had excellent design taste, and had the deep pockets of Ford Motor Company to back him up. Edsel made the Lincoln brand name one of the most respected in America. Edsel's death in 1943 put the Lincoln Division in a tailspin that lasted almost twenty years. *Credit: Ford Motor Company*

ernment would trouble the Lelands worse than the flintiest of their business associates.

The Lelands now had a superb modern factory, with nothing to make in it, and no clients. Surveying their position, Wilfred and Old Henry decided that it would be prudent to enter the automobile business again with a new car, one that would stand at the pinnacle of American craftsmanship and luxury. This new car would be called the Lincoln.

With growing enthusiasm and optimism, the Lelands amassed over $6 million of capital backing for their new venture, adding to it a million of their own money and signing notes for $3 million more. Based on their work at Cadillac and their experience with the Liberty engines, they created a novel 60deg side-valve V-8 to power the new cars and built several prototype chassis. Selecting the best of the chassis, they set about refining and perfecting their car until even old Henry Leland was pleased with the result.

The new Lincoln truly was a fine car for its day. Henry Leland said, "A thousandth of an inch is one-third the thickness of a human hair and ordinarily is regarded as a fine degree of accuracy. But dimensions of certain Lincoln parts are defined by measurements as fine as three-tenths of a thousandth, or about one-tenth the diameter of a human hair."

The first Lincoln was made on 130 or 136in wheelbases and called the Model L. Eight body styles were available, or the customer could order a bare chassis for custom coachwork. The car had a ladder-type frame, with a massive brace across the center and the perimeter narrowing toward the front of the car. Drive was delivered to the live rear axle via a torque tube; the front axle was solid. Semi-elliptic leaf springs were used all around, and brakes were cable activated drums on the rear wheels only. A typical tire size was 33x5in.

The first Lincoln V-8 displaced 357.8ci, or 5.8ltr. It used a single updraft carburetor, an automatic spark advance, and a multiplane crankshaft with five main bearings. Fitted to the crank were novel fork-and-blade connecting rods that performed the same balancing function as crankshaft counterweights, which had not yet appeared. Both intake and exhaust manifolds were on the inside of the V. Routing the exhaust downpipe right behind the dashboard was one of the Model L's few design flaws, although not a serious one. Cast-iron cylinder heads were removable and interchangeable. Pistons were cast from fine grain iron and matched closely to the size of the bores. Connecting rods were quite long (11in), which reduced scuffing force on the cylinder walls. The engine had a sealed cooling system with an overflow tank, similar to today's designs.

Roller-type valve lifters were actuated by a single, chain-driven camshaft. A nonsynchro three-speed transmission with standard H shift pattern took power from a dry, multiplate clutch and passed it back to a single-speed rear differential.

In all, it was a car to be expected from the Lelands: conservative in many respects, advanced in others, but finished with remarkable care and precision throughout. Directly after the war, quality materials were scarce and skilled labor rare. Despite their pioneering labor-friendly philosophy, the Lelands experienced numerous strikes and walk-outs while preparing the first Lincoln cars. Consequently, introduction of the Lincoln Model L was delayed for nearly nine months. When the Model L was conceived in 1919, the Leland's business plan called for the manufacture of 6,000 cars in the first year, with the number rising to 14,000 the following year. These fig-

This 1932 Lincoln has an unusual custom body by Brunn called the Double Entry Sports Sedan. Using a Victoria body style, this unique vehicle has a double-entry door on each side. The doors are hinged at both front and back and may be opened with either of two door handles. This car debuted at the New York Salon Show in November 1931. *Credit: Ford Motor Company*

ures were coined during the halcyon days of 1919, when the auto industry capered in a postwar boom.

Lincoln models ranged from a short wheelbase roadster and touring car at $4,500 to the limousine and town car at $6,600. The Lelands' clout with car buyers was so strong that 1,500 orders for the new cars came in (with deposits) before the first vehicles had been exhibited to the public. However, the autumn of 1920 saw a steep decline in the US economy. Car sales plunged from their 1919 levels. Sadly, Lincoln was caught in this crunch.

To further complicate matters, the US government suddenly made a claim against Lincoln Motors for over $5 million in taxes on war profits. This outrageous claim had little to do with the Lelands themselves but was actually a political football designed to enhance the careers of certain Washington politicians. Wilfred Leland went to Washington with a suitcase full of business records and, after a line-by-line disclosure of the Liberty engine ledgers, convinced tax examiners to cancel the outrageous assessment.

The first Lincolns were seen by the public in September 1920. In brief, these cars did not set the world on fire, although their quality was unmatched and undisputed. Slowly, word trickled in from the dealers that buyers thought the body styles were dated and unattractive. Indeed, the new Lincolns did look square and conservative. Neither of the Lelands had any sensitivity toward auto body design. For once, their conservativism had dealt the Lelands a serious blow. Only 700-some cars were sold in 1920, instead of the 6,000 that were projected. As a result, the new company was in financial trouble from the start.

Over the next two years, the Lelands, father and son, faced a mutinous board of directors, dealers who canceled orders en masse, and a constant battle to raise operating capital against weak sales.

In the course of those two stormy years, new body styles were mounted, some improvements were made to the car as a whole, and various creative financing ideas were floated. In the end, though, nothing could stop a long, sickening slide into receivership.

At this point, Henry Ford once again crossed paths with the Lelands. It would seem unlikely that the ultimate low-price manufacturer would link up with the ultimate prestige car maker, but that is exactly what happened.

Henry Ford is remembered as a tinkerer, mechanic extraordinaire, inventive genius, and one of the founding fathers of the automobile business worldwide. Ford's life and the dynasty he founded is well documented and needs little in the way of retelling here. But, as Ford looms large on Lincoln's horizon at this moment in history—1921 to 1922—it would be illuminating to examine several facets of Ford's career that bear on the fate of the Lincoln Motor Company.

Henry Ford, like Henry Leland, was a nineteenth century man who may have transformed the twentieth century but never seemed to truly embrace it. Ford began as a Michigan farm boy whose curiosity drove him to the big city of Detroit and led him to the great romance of his lifetime, the automobile. After working as an engineer at the Detroit Edison Company, Ford developed his hand-built Quadracycle, an impressive early automobile. Ford found financial backers to begin manufacture of his car, but then mysteriously ignored the company while he constructed a racer, the famous 999. After parting company with his first business, which was renamed Cadillac, Ford raised fresh capital and began a new automobile manufacturer in earnest, the Ford Motor Company. With mass production and the overwhelming sales of the famous Model T, the firm grew to become the largest privately owned business in history, and Ford became a cranky American Croesus.

Despite his mechanical brilliance, Henry Ford ruled his industrial empire like a Medici prince, favoring intrigue, social Darwinism, and even brutality. Ford constantly encouraged friction among his top executives, who were without fixed titles or job descriptions. From today's perspective, it's hard to imagine his tantrums, whims, and cruelties as the heart of a huge, multinational business with a commanding grip on its market.

In his labor relations, for example, Ford pioneered the $5-a-day wage; yet, he was also the man who had his "security" goons beat Walter Reuther and other United Auto Workers union organizers nearly to death, putting the mark of Cain on labor-management relations in the auto industry for decades to come.

By the early 1920s, Ford had amassed a fortune that has never been adequately counted. And he made most of it selling automobiles, the vast majority of them the famous, or infamous, Model T, the "Tin Lizzie."

When the Leland's rebellious board of directors voted to put the Lincoln Motor Company up for sale, Henry Ford was quoted in the Detroit press as saying that it would be a stain on the auto industry if the Le-

lands were allowed to go out of business. Was he sincere, or just laying the foundation for a brutal takeover? Again, it's unlikely that a conclusive answer can be reached, since all the principals in this drama (and their friends, confidantes, and children) are no longer living.

After the Lincoln board had voted to liquidate the company, Wilfred Leland worked like a demon to raise enough capital backing to recapture it. He failed. Plan B called for a friendly buy-out of the company, which would leave the Lelands in control; but no reliable money could be found.

Ford was one of those approached about buying Lincoln. William Emmons, Lelands' lawyer, contacted Ford through William Mayo, Ford's chief engineer. Ford reportedly said that he was cool on the idea but would think about it.

Wilfred Leland journeyed to New York in search of a $10 million loan, only to be told as he arrived that the government had again presented a tax claim against Lincoln for war profits (this time for $4.5 million). Now there was nothing left but to hope that Henry Ford could be persuaded to buy Lincoln and let the Lelands run their company in dignity.

In December 1921, Ford officially announced his decision to buy Lincoln. His first offer was for $5 million, although that was later raised to $8 million. By the time Ford had finished paying the government's tax bill, which had been mysteriously reduced to $500,000, and paying the major creditors, he spent about $12 million to complete the takeover. The sale was finalized on February 4, 1922, and Ford's check for $8 million was presented to the receivers on February 11.

But those who thought the Leland's troubles were finally over had guessed wrong. Within two weeks of his purchase, Henry Ford sent Charles Sorensen, the ruthless head of production at the Rouge River plant, and engineer William B. Mayo into the Lincoln factory. A few days later, a small army of workers arrived to begin making "improvements." The hard fact was that Ford now owned Lincoln, and he planned to take the rough-and-tumble Ford ideas and apply them to Lincoln, rather than take the Lelands' precision ideas and apply them to the Ford operation.

When the Lelands objected to this policy, they found themselves in a curious position. Wilfred visited Ford at his Dearborn home, Fair Lane, where Henry Ford told Wilfred that, if those new managers bothered him, to just "whack 'em. Don't let 'em do it!"

Whacking was clearly not in the Leland vocabulary. As spring wore on, the friction increased. By June

Representing more contemporary styling, the Zephyr line from Lincoln was an attempt to reach a more middle-class buyer with the Lincoln name. It was a successful attempt, too. This 1940 three-window coupe is typical of Zephyr's styling with its pontoon fenders and large-radius curves. It must have had a huge trunk. *Credit: Ford Motor Company*

The Continental began as a one-off prototype for Edsel's personal use; but Edsel was so mobbed on his Florida vacation with orders for the Continental, it became a pro- duction car. This 1940 Continental may have been a hand- built preproduction vehicle. *Credit: Ford Motor Company*

1922, it was all over. Ford sent Ernest G. Liebold and William B. Mayo to see the younger Leland. "You bet- ter go over and tell Wilfred we don't want him any more," Henry Ford reportedly told his men, according to the book *Master of Precision*.

A Ford press release said that the Lelands had re- signed. Other than a check for $363,000 that Ford had given the elder Leland for his stock when the sale of the company took place, the Lelands were never compen- sated further by Ford for their part in creating and man- aging Lincoln. While the Lelands had been playing a genteel game of croquet, Ford was pitching hardball.

Yet, from the perspective of the auto enthusiast, there is no doubt that Ford saved the Lincoln car from extinction. The Lelands had proved rather conclusively that they couldn't run the financial side of their own company, and thus, had lost it. Under Ford's umbrella, Lincoln could be expected to weather any hard time that might lie ahead. Old Henry Leland, the mechani-

cal genius, was near the end of his life. Wilfred might have been able to manage the business, but he could never have supplied the engineering talent that Ford had in abundance.

Immediate changes to the Model L were few. Ford substituted aluminum pistons for cast-iron and devel- oped a thermo-siphon cooling system—which made the cars prone to overheating. Overall, though, the me- chanical condition of the Lincoln under Ford remained almost identical to the Leland product.

One large departure was the dismantling of Lin- coln's sales network. Lincolns would now be sold through Ford dealerships. A total of 5,626 cars were shipped to dealers in 1922, a number remarkably close to the 6,000 the Lelands had forecast in 1919. Through the mid-1920s, Lincoln shipped between seven and eight thousand cars a year, and that number decreased only in the early 1930s as the Great Depression rattled the country's financial strength.

Another important change was the creation of new bodies for the continuing Model L. When the Lelands exited, Edsel Ford became president of the Lincoln division of the Ford Motor Company. Edsel had an excellent visual sense and was a tolerable auto stylist on his own. He commissioned some of the United States' leading coachbuilders to revamp the Lincoln's dull looks. The results were excellent. Firms such as Dietrich, Fleetwood, LeBaron, Brunn, and others all made Lincoln bodies under the new Ford regime.

Perhaps it is only a coincidence, perhaps it is fate, but in Edsel Ford the Lincoln marque found the ideal person to bring it to perfection. The already advanced engineering of the Lelands needed only to be wrapped in the kind of elegant and attractive bodywork that would give Lincoln distinction and stature. Edsel was exactly the man to do it.

At roughly this time, Lincolns became associated with American presidents. According to some recently questioned records, Calvin Coolidge ordered the first of a long succession of presidential Lincolns. It was a 1924 LeBaron-bodied touring sedan, delivered to the White House motor pool in December 1923. Unlike the presidential cars of today, this machine was almost entirely stock, including heavy, wood-spoked "artillery" wheels. Coolidge used the car for the duration of his term, then passed it on to Herbert Hoover.

Production of the Model L continued through the Roaring '20s. Body styles proliferated, from tidy runabouts on the small wheelbase, to grand limousines on the larger chassis.

Along with US presidents, the Lincoln Model L was the chosen transportation of Prohibition-era gangsters. Bootleggers favored the car for its style, speed, and handling. The Capone mob in Chicago was especially fond of Lincolns. If you envision a gangster leaning out of a big 1920s car, spraying his enemies with hot lead from a Thompson submachine gun, that car was most likely a Lincoln.

Not to be outdone, law enforcement agencies ordered Lincolns as well. Lincoln built a special version called the Police Flyer that featured a highly tuned engine and four-wheel brakes. As a result of the success of the Police Flyers, four-wheel brakes became available to the public in 1927. They were, however, still cable operated. As he aged, Henry Ford became increasingly suspicious of any mechanical innovation, and he still had the last word about Lincoln engineering, whether Edsel was titular head of the company or not.

The Lincoln greyhound radiator cap ornament first appeared in 1925. Edsel wanted to give Lincoln an identity to match the great marques of the era, such as Hispano-Suisa, Rolls Royce, Cadillac, and Packard. The lithe and elegant greyhound, caught fully extended in the midst of a running stride, captured the speed and grace for which Lincolns were already known and added another icon to the growing Lincoln legend. The original design for the greyhound was commissioned by Edsel from the Gorham Company in Rhode Island.

Throughout the 1920s, Lincoln endeavored to stay even with or exceed its competition. Small, incremental improvements, such as the addition of four-wheel brakes, continued. Indeed, the Lincoln factory claimed that there "were no model years" in the standard sense. But, by the late '20s, it was clear the car needed more power to adequately handle the massive coachbuilt bodies that were increasingly mounted on its chassis.

In 1928, the L engine was subjected to its first major update. It was bored out to 3.5in (from 3.375in), increasing displacement to 384.8ci. Larger valves were fitted and the combustion chamber reshaped for a stronger burn. Compression was increased modestly to 4.81:1, and conical valve springs were added to handle the higher cylinder pressures. A counterbalanced crankshaft completed the refit. At the same time, the exhaust system was rerouted, eliminating the dashboard hot spot that often bothered front seat passengers. However, the new, more powerful engine did not run in the whisper-quiet, vibration-free manner of the Leland V-8.

Lincoln advertising of the period emphasized color and style at a time when Fords were still painted mostly in black—one reason the Model T was seen as more and more of an antique.

In 1931, a new Lincoln model, the K, was introduced. This model was an evolution of the Model L and featured a 145in wheelbase and revamped engine. Increased compression (4.95:1), a Stromberg downdraft carburetor, and extended valve timing raised the engine's output to 120hp at 2900rpm. Both the engine and the passenger seating areas were lowered in the new chassis to give coachbuilders a lower and longer profile with which to work.

The greatest changes in Lincoln history to this point came in 1932 with the development of the KA and KB models. The KA was a return to the shorter wheelbase chassis, using the new K V-8 engine. But the KB used the long wheelbase chassis in conjunction with a massive and magnificent new V-12 engine, based on the existing K V-8.

The Lincoln V-12 displaced 447.9ci. It was a 65deg V engine with a 3.25x4.5in bore and stroke. Compression was slightly lower than the V-8 at 4.5:1. This 150hp engine was mated to Lincoln's new "free-wheeling" transmission, which it shared with the KA model.

The new V-12 was necessary to compete with similar engines from Duesenberg, Packard, and Auburn, and of course Cadillac's V-16. But the split into two distinct product lines, a lower and a higher, was a response to the growing economic chaos of the Great Depression. By 1932, it was clear that the US economy was not going to rebound quickly from the disastrous stock market crash of 1929. As millions of Americans lost their jobs in factory closings, the number of wealthy customers plummeted, making the market for top luxury cars smaller and more competitive than ever.

Hollywood stars, a few smokestack moguls, and those with old money on the East Coast and burgeoning oil money in the West could still afford to buy the very best in automotive hardware and have the finest coachbuilt bodies fitted to them, but their numbers were dwindling fast. Some of the leading luxury car manufacturers eventually closed their shops and vanished into history. If Lincoln had not been part of the Ford colossus, it most likely would have become extinct as well.

During 1932, sales of both new Lincoln models came to only 3,388 units. Clearly the harsh economic times were decapitating the luxury car market. Ironically, coachbuilders such as Brunn and Murray produced some of the most exciting Lincoln bodies seen to date. The Sport runabout convertibles of 1932 were elegant and racy, capturing the essence of that wild era perfectly. Sadly, Murray produced only three of its Lincoln roadster bodies before closing its doors forever, signaling to some the end of the custom-built era. Indeed, that time was rapidly coming to a close.

Not surprisingly, in 1933, Lincoln introduced a smaller, 125hp V-12 to power the KA chassis. This completely new, 67deg V, side-valve engine displaced 381.7ci from a 3.00x4.50in bore and stroke. It was a more modern engine than the KB V-12, with roller tappets, bronze bearings, and a self-lashing accessory drive chain.

Both the KA and KB chassis were changed from the ladder style to an X-frame design, with the 136 and 145in wheelbases retained for this model year. Yet as the Depression continued to worsen, sales continued to slide, reaching a new low of 1,998 units for 1933.

By 1934, other changes occurred in Lincoln hardware. A new V-12 engine was produced, combining many of the elements and virtues of the two previous twelves. The new engine was a 67deg V that displaced 414ci and produced 150hp. This motor was larger than the previous V-12s and had aluminum cylinder heads with improved combustion chamber design, although they were again L-heads.

These new cars were known as Series K and featured radiators with a slight rearward tilt at the top for both the 136 and 145in wheelbases. The smaller Lincolns were all equipped with production bodies by Murray and others while the 145in wheelbase cars were special order only. Sales for 1934 indicated an upturn of interest in the new line-up at 2,450 units.

In 1935, Lincoln again changed its model designations, calling the 136in wheelbase the Series 301 and the 145in wheelbase the Series 514. Along with those two, a new 160in commercial chassis was introduced for applications such as ambulances, hearses, and delivery vehicles. The dim beginning of cab-forward design was visible in Lincolns of this time. Their center of gravity was lowered, and the front seats were moved forward 11in. This forward move was aided by a new engine mounting system. It used five rubber isolation mounts and pushed the pedals and other control hardware forward as well. The cars routinely rode on 17x17.50 tires. A new presidential Lincoln was delivered that year, a seven-passenger Model 302 touring car with custom leather upholstery, for use by Franklin D. Roosevelt.

The really big news in 1935 was the development of a completely new "small" Lincoln, the Zephyr. This radical vehicle was based on the stunning Zephyr show car designed by Tom Tjaarda and adapted for production by Bob Gregorie. The original Zephyr was a streamlined, unibody, rear-engine concept car that had caused quite a stir at the Chicago Century of Progress exhibition. Premiering in November 1935 as a '36 model, the production Zephyr was powered by a front-mounted V-12 and employed unit-body construction on a 122in wheelbase, with 202in overall length.

Sleek and aerodynamic, the Zephyr did what the Chrysler Airflow couldn't; it brought new streamlined styling to a public whose tastes were changing with hitherto unknown speed. The Zephyr Model 902 four-door and Model 903 two-door bodies were manufactured by the Briggs Body Company for Lincoln. Transverse front and rear leaf springs were an obvious Ford touch. The Zephyr was fitted with 16x7.00 tires on heavy-spoked wheels, which it shared with the Ford V-8. Powering the new Zephyr was another all new V-12 engine. It displaced 267ci from a 2.75x3.75in bore and stroke, and was conservatively rated at 110hp. It was, in fact, a Ford V-8 and a half. Such a powerplant was fitting for the Zephyr, the first mass-produced Lincoln and a car that sought to bridge the gap between Ford and Lincoln products, engineering, and markets. Production of the new Zephyr reached an astounding 15,000 units for 1936 while only about 1,500 of the larger Lincolns were delivered.

In 1937, a three-passenger Zephyr coupe, Model 720, was added to the line-up. In all, nearly 20,000 Zephyrs were delivered in 1937, proving the soundness of the car's concept and the public's enthusiastic reaction to its innovative shape.

The following year saw a mild restyle for the Zephyr and a number of mechanical refinements. In addition, the first Zephyr convertibles were produced, in both two- and four-door styles. The car was also lengthened slightly to improve passenger room, and the floor was lowered over an inch thanks to a new rear differential design. Zephyr sales in 1938 were slightly off at 19,000 units, but only about 430 of the big Lincolns were made that year, all but 200 of which were shipped with factory bodies. As the Depression ground on, it was increasingly clear that the age of the huge, custom-built luxury car was forever past.

Another alarming trend in the late 1930s was the rise of fascism in Europe, namely Francisco Franco in Spain, Benito Mussolini in Italy, and Adolph Hitler in Germany. While most Americans felt, as they had in 1917, that the United States didn't belong in a European war, President Roosevelt and others realized that the combination of fascism in Europe, Japanese empire building in Asia, and Communism in Russia could surround the United States with unfriendly global neighbors in the decades to come.

When Hitler invaded Poland and triggered World War II in 1939, the United States remained neutral, though clearly siding with the Allies in principle. The Japanese attack on Pearl Harbor in December 1941 (using Mitsubishi-built "Zero" fighter-bombers) finally catapulted the United States into war, both in Europe and across the Pacific.

Yet, for all the terror and turmoil of the late 1930s, a new Lincoln emerged from these dark days that was to help define the company's image over the next decade. This model would become one of the best known and most recognizable nameplates in America—the Continental.

Thank Edsel Ford for the Continental. As the head of Lincoln, Edsel occasionally had custom cars made for his winter vacations in Florida or his summer trips to Maine, both unfortunate seasons in the Detroit climate.

In 1939, Edsel combined a Zephyr body and a Ford V-8 to create the Mercury, which occupied a price position between those cars as well. But Edsel wanted another car, a sportier model at the top of the Mercury line. Resistance from Ford executives determined him to place his concept as a Lincoln.

Edsel had long been close with one of his leading designers, Eugene Turenne "Bob" Gregorie. The son of a wealthy plantation owner, Gregorie had been a yacht designer and had penned custom bodies for Rolls-Royce chassis before coming to work for Ford. He was an upper-class gentleman with whom Edsel felt comfortable enough to speak from his inner self. Edsel Ford and Gregorie would spend hours in the styling studios discussing design elements and comparing the European cars they both admired. Their discussions led to the idea of making a special one-off for Edsel from a Zephyr convertible coupe, a car that would be "continental" in its elegance and sporty character.

In 1938, Gregorie began sketching a proposal for this car. It would have a long hood, smoothly stretched semipontoon fenders, and a convertible top with blind rear quarters. At the rear, an exposed spare tire carrier and rounded trunk would be the focus of attention. That external spare tire carrier would become the signature of the Continental, and a vestige of it still remains today.

By the end of '38 a 1/10th scale clay model had been finished. The Continental was similar to the stock Zephyr, but the body was lowered 3in and the hood lengthened 12in. The original Continental prototype was a heavyweight lead sled, and, according to Edsel, it leaked badly around the fittings of the convertible top.

The original Continental was delivered to Edsel in Florida in March 1939 and caused a stir wherever it went. Edsel personally recorded nearly 200 orders for the Continental and then returned to Detroit ready to produce the car in a limited run of 500. Later in '39, two additional prototypes were built, now with the idea of preparing the car for production.

The new prototypes kept many of the lines and dimensions of the original car; the hood was stretched only 8in over stock, and the trunk was raised to balance the hood. Rear fender skirts were retained. An assembly line

The Lincoln Continental Mark I
Built by Ford Motor Company in 1940
V-12 engine, 120 HP
Wheelbase 125 inches

was constructed in parallel to the Zephyr line, and by the end of the year twenty-five Continentals had been built.

The 1940 Continental was beautiful. From its Frenched-in headlamps and ship's-prow hood to the strong lines of the rag-top and the distinctive bump of the exposed spare at the back, it was as lovely a car as the period produced. Although the K V-12 engine was not the best powerplant ever, it still gave the Continental distinction and excellent power.

Inside, the first Continentals had bench front and rear seats, a unique central instrument cluster (although many components were shared with the production Zephyr), leather seats, and leather door panels.

The first hardtop Continental, or Coupe, was pro-

nental (now a separate line of its own), and the large Custom, a Zephyr-styled vestige of the big K models. The major change for that year was the introduction of the Liquamatic automatic transmission, a complex three-speed semiautomatic gearbox that retained a manual clutch behind the torque converter and allowed use of overdrive in second and third gears, under manual control.

With the entry of the United States into World War II, the federal government ordered US auto makers to suspend car production for the duration and convert their factories to making war materiel. The last Lincoln produced in the prewar era came off the assembly line at the end of February 1942. It would be 1945 before new Lincolns were again available for sale. By then, Lincoln's champion Edsel Ford had died—worn out, some would say, from the stress and strain of dealing with his aging, tyrannical, and increasingly capricious father. Lincoln's greatest challenges were yet to come.

duced in 1940. It looked a little more sedate than the convertible, but was still a handsome car for the times. About 400 Continentals were made that year, and it seemed obvious that the Continental would go far beyond the original limited run of 500 units that Edsel had planned at the start.

In 1941, Lincoln offered the Zephyr, the Conti-

Chapter 2

Seeking a New Self—The 1940s and 1950s

While young Americans donned khaki uniforms and spilled their blood across Europe and the Pacific, Lincoln factories produced Jeeps and massive dohc engines for Sherman tanks. Gearing up Lincoln plants for wartime production was mandated by law, but it was also a fitting nod to the past, like Henry Leland's patriotic manufacture of Liberty aircraft engines during World War I.

The decades after World War II were an era of great change and uncertainty at Lincoln. Complicating matters, postwar America no longer provided an easy market for high-end luxury cars like the elegant Model K. Despite Lincoln's undeniable success with the lower-priced Zephyr line in the late 1930s, the future was by no means secure. New managers groped their way for-

Rushed into production at the end of 1945, these '46 Lincolns are similar to the prewar cars, but with some differences in chrome trim and bumpers. *Credit: Ford Motor Company*

This 1946 Continental continues with the extensive sheet metal changes of 1942, but it has a more massive grille and bumpers with lengthened, flat-top fenders. *Credit: Ford Motor Company*

ward, trying to balance the evolving tastes of a car-hungry America with powerful competition from Packard, Chrysler Imperial, Cadillac, and other GM brands. For Lincoln, it was as though the war never ended but shifted from the trenches of France and Iwo Jima to those of Dearborn and Detroit.

Lincoln suffered a devastating loss in wartime. The untimely death of Edsel Ford in May 1943 left Lincoln with a leadership vacuum and Ford Motor Company without a crown prince. Poor Edsel. His nervous stomach and sensitive disposition finally overwhelmed him. He left behind a grieving widow, three sons, a daughter, and a luxury car division that had no clear vision of what to do with itself. E.T. Gregorie, the stylist, then resigned, unable to face Lincoln without Edsel in charge. Old Henry Ford finally retired in September 1945, world weary and dottering.

Now both Lincoln and the entire Ford Motor

This 1951 Cosmopolitan Sport Sedan is typical of the new envelope bodies for Lincoln in the 1950s. This particular car was used as a model for the Lincoln Accessories Catalog that year, which explains the rarely ordered spotlight on the driver's side A-pillar. *Credit: Ford Motor Company*

Company needed a new leader, the question was: who? Within Ford, a power struggle had simmered for years. Old Henry Ford grew increasingly dependent on Harry Bennett, the ex-boxer and thug who had been his "head of security" and all around bag-man. More than once, Ford mentioned that, in the absence of Edsel, he might like Bennett to take control of the company after he retired. This sentiment brought an understandable tremor of dread to senior executives and managers. Charles Sorensen, the baron of the Rouge River plant, an immense power within Ford and one of Henry Ford's oldest cronies, also thought that he might catch the crown at Ford.

Ultimately, neither man would prevail. Henry Ford II, Edsel's oldest son, returned early from military service and declared himself available for the top job, even though old Henry didn't especially like the lad. When he reported for work, Henry II was given little respect around the Ford plant; he was even brushed-off by Bennett. The three-way struggle between Henry II, Bennett, and Sorensen dragged on for months while many seasoned executives either jumped ship or were unceremoniously axed by one of the three contenders.

Surprisingly, in the end it was the Ford women who played king maker. They insisted that family prevail and Henry II become the president of the company. Eleanor Clay Ford, Edsel's widow, threatened old Henry with the sale of her 41 percent of Ford stock, a move that would throw the company into the hands of strangers. Henry's wife, Clara Ford, stood with her grandson. Reluctantly, angrily, the old man capitulated, and the younger Ford was voted into control. At last, Henry II had the authority. Sorensen, intending a power play, threatened to resign and was shocked when old Henry Ford simply shook his hand and told him to enjoy retirement. Bennett was sent packing by John Bugas, a former FBI agent who faced Bennett down in Bennett's own office, both of them with drawn pistols!

Now what of the future? Not unlike Shakespeare's Prince Hal, young Henry II was known as a spoiled rich

After so much waiting and fussing, the new Lincoln and the Lincoln Cosmopolitan for 1949 represent the Mercury designs that were "promoted" to be Lincoln models. While the cars were sleek and contemporary, Ford and Lincoln managers didn't like what they called the "frowning" front grille. Although the Lincoln and Cosmo look very similar in this illustration, the Lincoln is a true notchback while the Cosmo is closer to a fastback design. *Credit: Alonzo Merkin Collection*

kid. Few thought he had the guts to lead the empire he had inherited. But, like his fabled granddad, there was much more to "Hank the Deuce" than met the eye.

Two immediate challenges faced Henry II: bringing out a postwar car line and moving from the chaotic and undisciplined vest-pocket business practices of old Henry to a modern corporate structure. The first and most pressing problem was to get the new model year underway while the development of future models proceeded.

Those Lincolns that became available in July 1945 as 1946-47 cars were recycled 1942 models with minor trim updates involving bumpers and grille—easy to change cosmetics. The upcoming model year, 1948, would see the first all-new Fords, Mercurys and Lincolns since before the war.

In a move that would herald Ford's plans to challenge GM as a full-spectrum auto maker, Lincoln was detached from the Ford Motor Company in a Lincoln-

Two Sturdy New Chassis

Nothing revolutionary about the chassis of the 1949 Lincolns, just good solid, strong steel. The "X"- braced frame and live rear axle were just about universal in the US at that time and continued as the dominant chassis layout until well into the 1960s. Note all the body mounting points on the side of the near frame rail. *Credit: Alonzo Merkin Collection*

Mercury Division. Thomas Skinner was appointed the new head of Lincoln.

Not only did Henry Ford II need to purge the many Harry Bennett stooges from the company, but he needed to assert his position in a corporation, indeed an industry, where toughness had always been a major virtue. Ford did both in a single swoop, hiring an almost completely new team of upper managers. Known as the "Whiz Kids," they were a group of ten World War II Army Air Corps veterans who stuck together after the armistice and shopped their talents as a team. It happened that Ford needed a group with experience, and internal trust, and communication as a package deal. Loyal only to Henry Ford II, these new managers spread throughout the company, with some of them climbing to the highest executive positions.

Consisting of Charles B. "Tex" Thornton, Francis C. "Jack" Reith, Robert S. McNamara, Arjay Miller, Ben Mills, George Moore, and others, the former logistics officers became the centerpiece of Ford's new corporate leadership. However, because this team had never worked for a major industrial concern before, Henry II hired Ernest R. Breech as the new corporate vice-president. Breech had been president of Bendix Aviation and could claim GM's Alfred Sloan as his mentor.

With the ascension of Edsel's son Henry Ford II to power, E.T. "Bob" Gregorie returned to the fold, to become chief stylist for all of Ford Motor Company. Now they were ready to go.

As an omen of this new era at Lincoln and Ford, the Continental Cabriolet was picked to be the pace car for the triumphal 1946 Indianapolis 500.

The 1946 Lincoln line-up did see some nomenclature changes. The Custom was discontinued and the Zephyr name dropped, making all Zephyr models Lincolns. Only the Continental name continued on as before the war. With widespread labor unrest and serious shortages of materials throughout the auto industry, Lincoln output was not strong, despite the avid demand for cars. Production for 1946 reached slightly over 16,500 vehicles altogether. Prices ranged from $2,318 for a Lincoln Club Coupe to $4,476 for a Continental Cabriolet.

On a human note, old Henry Ford died on April 7th, 1947, after viewing floods around the city of Dearborn and seeing his beloved Fair Lane powerhouse go off-line. The eighty-three-year-old man passed quietly in the night, held tightly by his wife, Clara. The next day, the automobile business felt not only the passing of a giant but faced the sudden, sobering thought that the

Look at *Lincoln* for 1949

The Lincoln Cosmopolitan

Nothing could be finer — or newer

The Lincoln

LITHO IN U.S.A.

For 1949, the Lincoln name was shunted to the smaller 121in wheelbase chassis while the Cosmopolitan became the larger, top-of-the-line car. Both were available in sever- al models including a premium convertible Cosmopolitan. *Credit: Alonzo Merkin Collection*

American century was now nearly half over.

Due to the chaos of corporate restructuring and a lack of consensus on how the next generation of Lincolns should look, the 1947 cars were little more than carryovers from the already dated '42—'46 vehicles— as was most of Detroit's output at that time. The big year would be 1948. Even with the enormous postwar demand for cars, those at Ford and Lincoln-Mercury had a sense that 1948 could be a make-or-break year for the company.

Despite these hopes and expectations, there would be no grandiose new model year for Lincoln in 1948. Management was still squabbling about the appearance of the cars and how heavy they should be. Further complicating the picture was GM's ravenous appetite for steel and tooling. Ford simply couldn't acquire enough raw materials to create the dies and patterns for all of its new cars.

An announcement delivered to the press said tersely that the 1948 model year would begin in November

The most popular Lincoln in 1951 was this Type 74 Lincoln Sports Sedan; 12,279 of these cars sold for $2,796 each. *Credit: Ford Motor Company*

This sleek and attractive car is a 1951 Lincoln Cosmopolitan Six-Passenger convertible. It was the most expensive Lincoln in its model year at $4,234. Lincoln made extensive modifications to its V-8 engine in 1951, increasing horsepower and improving reliability. *Credit: Ford Motor Company*

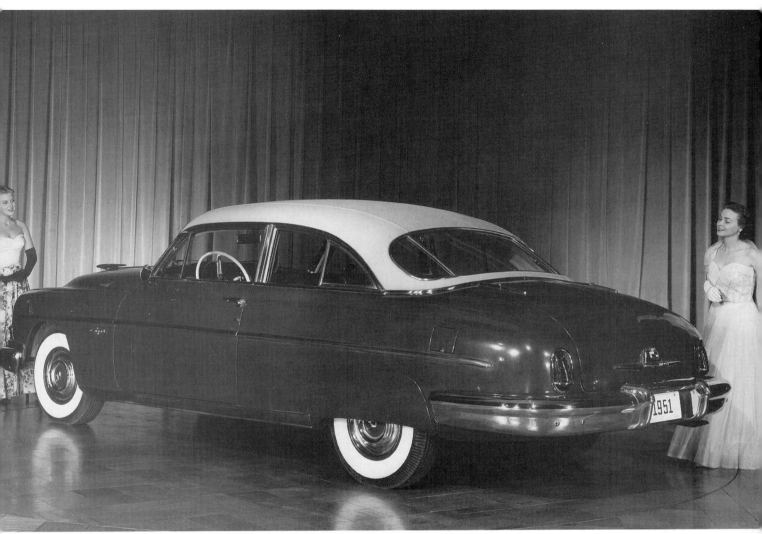

The 1951 Capri Six-Passenger Coupe was available in three colors and a choice of either leather or leather and Bedford Cord upholstery. Like the exterior, the instrument panel is also two-toned. *Credit: Ford Motor Company*

1947, but the cars would be the same. One significant change was the appointment of Henry II's brother, Benson Ford, as general manager of the Lincoln-Mercury Division, replacing Thomas Skinner.

The new products finally made their debut in April 1948 as the first domestic 1949 models. One surprise was an entirely new top-of-the-line vehicle, the Cosmopolitan, with the name Lincoln downshifted to the previous Zephyr-sized car. The Continental was finally discontinued. Instead of competing with Packard, Duesenberg, and Cadillac, the Lincoln nameplate was now more of a rival for Buick and Oldsmobile. Lo, how the mighty had fallen. A 1949 Lincoln Sport Sedan sold for $2,574, and the Cosmopolitan Sport Sedan cost $3,238.

There is, of course, a story behind Lincoln's down-market shift. The postwar years saw the rise of the great American middle class. While the numbers of the extremely wealthy had rapidly declined throughout the Depression years, the ranks of the upper-middle class continued to grow. It was to these folks that the former top-end luxury car companies now addressed themselves. And it was with these buyers that the name "Lincoln" was expected to have an almost mystical appeal. But there was another element.

At some point, late in the development cycle, when Henry Ford II and Ernest Breech saw Bob Gregorie's designs for the new Fords and Mercurys, they thought them too big, too bulky. Yet a substantial amount of

The front of this 1952 Lincoln Capri Special Custom convertible is completely different than that of the '49 to '51 cars. The headlights now protrude, and the face has a "Pontiac" look to it. This car was the high-dollar machine from Lincoln in 1952. It cost $4,025, and 1,191 were sold. The convertible top worked electrically, with "one push of a button." *Credit: Ford Motor Company*

money had already been invested in the tooling for these products. Ford couldn't simply walk away from them. So, to make a long story short, the Ford design was promoted to a Mercury and the Mercury to a Lincoln. The Lincoln designs were unceremoniously abandoned. With them went any sense of continuity for the marque. When a design competition for the new Ford car line was won by George Walker, an outside stylist, Bob Gregorie again resigned, this time for good.

The new Cosmopolitan rode on a 125in wheelbase and offered four body styles: coupe, four-door fastback Town Sedan, notchback Sport Sedan, and convertible. They were joined by 121in wheelbase Lincolns offering the same models except the fastback.

Overall, the Cosmopolitan was a good-looking, modern car, but one with several peculiarities. It was a long and large car, with a slab-sided body style not shared with any other Ford product. It had a rounded "bathtub" look that was sleek and streamlined, and had very little of the chrome trim that would disgrace domestic cars in only a few years. Engineering advances included new coil-spring independent front suspen-

Hardtop styling came to Lincoln with this Capri Special Custom Coupe. According to the press release for this car, it had a ". . . new 160 horsepower, overhead valve V-8 engine, a rugged X-type frame, a unique [ball-joint] front suspension and suspended foot pedals. . . ." *Credit: Ford Motor Company*

sions, Hotchkiss drive rear ends, and reworked frames—all big steps for the highly conservative Ford Motor Company.

Interestingly enough, these Cosmopolitans don't look very big in pictures, even when a model stands with them. But come upon one of them in person, and you will be surprised by just how large and spacious they are.

The front end was certainly the most curious aspect of the '49 Lincolns and Cosmopolitans. First, they had grilles in the shape of a wide, downturned V. Many Ford executives thought it gave them a "frowning" appearance. Also, these cars' headlamps were set back, or Frenched, into the front fenders. This might have seemed a deliberate styling element, but it wasn't. Original plans called for shuttered headlamps, with small doors that rotated down and covered them in the daytime hours for an effect similar to the Cord 810 or the '42 DeSoto. Then at the last minute, body engineers declared that they couldn't make the headlight doors work. Styling had to quickly incorporate recessed headlamps. Their solution was a minitunnel effect that is a signature of Lincolns from this period. Due to the frowning grille and deep-set eyes, the Cosmopolitan was familiarly known as the "water buffalo," a name without much affection.

Inside, the 1949 Lincoln and Cosmopolitan were well appointed but plain. Both cars featured heavily padded bench seating for six and had very simple dashboards and wide, thin-rim steering wheels. Leather was available as an interior option and was standard in the Cosmopolitan convertible.

The Cosmopolitans and 1949 Lincolns debuted with a new V-8, which was an improvement from the pesky V-12 of the Zephyr, but more of a step sideways than forward. The new motor was a typical Ford flathead, side-valve engine. It had been designed for rugged use and was first put in 1948 Ford F-100 trucks. The ample torque of this engine was welcomed by Lincoln drivers, but Lincoln salesmen were not pleased at having to sell against the high-compression overhead-valve engine introduced by Cadillac for 1949 or the ohv Chrysler Hemi, which debuted for 1951.

Problems with the new Lincoln engine surfaced

29

Henry Ford II looks calm and confident in the mid-1950s. He actually seems to be enjoying himself in a preproduction Thunderbird. *Credit: Ford Motor Company*

fairly soon and led to some midyear modifications that included revising how the engine blocks were cast, plus a change from three to four piston rings per cylinder. However, the real problem was that the crankshaft and the engine were out of balance to each other. This would take longer to solve. Unfortunately, it led to the new Lincolns having a poor reputation for reliability. Other gripes about this model year included hard steering and interior water leaks from the heater.

Despite these flaws, buyers liked the new Lincolns and purchased them avidly. Sales figures for the lengthy 1949 model year show over 73,000 cars sold by the division—with Lincoln about 3,000 vehicles ahead of Cosmopolitan, overall.

Only superficial changes were made for the 1950 model year, although a number of fixes addressed the more prominent weaknesses of the '49s. The frowning grille that gave the '49 cars their water buffalo face became straight, but the cars lost some of their uniqueness in the process. Now they looked like improbable, wide-mouthed sea creatures, but at least upper management was happy.

Other modifications for 1950 included a fix to the hard steering that plagued the '49s. The steering problem was remedied through a change in the steering box. A new, direct-pull parking brake appeared, and new motor mounts attempted to reduce engine vibration. The Lincoln received a new rear window that was larger than in the past, almost 1000sq-in of glass. New bumpers were less toothsome, and the "airplane" hood ornament was larger than before.

Two new Lincolns showed up in midyear 1950, both luxury versions of existing coupe models. The

Notice the three-piece backlight on this type 73A Cosmopolitan Custom Sedan. All Lincolns in 1952 had them, except convertibles. *Credit: Ford Motor Company*

Lido was the new top-of-the-line Lincoln coupe, the Capri a deluxe Cosmopolitan coupe. The Capri represented a step toward hardtop styling, but neither car was a true hardtop. Both models featured a heightened level of trim with vinyl-covered tops, sumptuous interiors, and elegant seats upholstered in the finest fabrics and softest leathers. The Lido was priced at $2,720 and the Capri at $3,045.

In case you're not familiar with the term "hardtop," it refers to a body design that makes a permanent steel top look as though it's a convertible. The hardtop has the slender A-pillar and absent B-pillar of a convertible and a top of minimal profile. The hardtop body is a by-product of advanced engineering, requiring excellent styling, superior metallurgy, and first-rate body/chassis integration. Only in the post-World War II era was the domestic industry sophisticated enough to mass produce such elegant and attractive bodies. In this, as in many other technical features, Cadillac was the industry leader, and Lincoln lagged behind.

However, in marketing terms, the 1950 Lincolns were a substantial success. The introduction of the Capri and the Lido marked a move back upscale to where Lincoln really belonged. At that level the cars were now selling very well, and were perceived as true quality, true luxury products.

Overall, 1950 marked a downturn for the domestic car industry. The start of the Korean War saw new shortages of raw materials and increased Cold War tensions. Not only were American GIs under arms again so soon after World War II, but the involvement of Red China and Russia in the conflict led to fears of World War III and a possible nuclear apocalypse. It was not a time of buyer confidence.

For 1951, incremental changes were made to the basic 1949 cars. The Lincolns received a styling update at the rear end including new taillights and bigger rear windows. Structural additions were fashioned at the back of the cars to support the larger glass area. Similar but less extensive changes were made to the Cosmopolitan models. Lincoln-like "spear" side moldings were added to the Cosmos in an attempt to reduce their visual bulk, and new tail lights appeared. New wheel covers graced the entire line-up.

Inside, a number of changes were made to update the interiors of both model lines. New colors and fabrics complimented a change in switch gear, steering wheels, and other interior hardware. A non-glare

31

Combining hardtop and sedan styling in a slightly top-heavy package is this 1953 Cosmopolitan four-door sedan. *Credit: Ford Motor Company*

rearview mirror was added, and a new dome light configuration was used. Sales of the standard Lincoln were marginally down for 1951, but the Cosmos were very strong, selling almost 50 percent more units than the previous year.

In 1952, a totally new line of Lincolns appeared. These were the second generation of vehicles developed under Henry Ford II's leadership of the company—and they were worth the wait. The new vehicles were completely redesigned, with newer, vastly better chassis and the very first ohv V-8 ever to sit in a Lincoln body. The new cars were called Lincoln Capri and Lincoln Cosmopolitan. Each was offered as a four-door sedan, a two-door hardtop coupe, and a Capri Custom convertible at the very top-of-the-line.

Remarkably, these cars were slightly smaller than the models they replaced. They rode on a 123in wheelbase, directly between the 121in Capri and the 125in Cosmopolitan of the previous year. While the design of the new Cosmopolitan and Capri seemed to be a melange of features from Cadillac and Chrysler, it was an elegant piece of work and retains much of its freshness today. As a side note, the headlamps of this new vehicle thrust out from the body, in a complete reversal of the previous, involuted design.

The new body style was more aggressively modern than any postwar Lincoln product. The greenhouse was enlarged, with about 20 percent more glass area, and it better balanced the overall size of the body, making for a more harmonious whole. The design featured a heavy-side concept, with slightly curving flanks, and a forward-angled chrome bar on a stylized rear fender air intake. Mercurys had only half a bar. The front bumper featured dual conical spinners (often called "dagmars" after a busty Swedish film starlet) and mostly concealed the grille, which had no decorative cover.

The new chassis looked to be a winner, and so it would be in the Mexican road race, the Carrera Panamericana, an international race held in the 1950s. Some of its outstanding features were an all-new frame with six cross-members for increased torsional stiffness, additional K braces, centered engine mounts, 11in brake drums, stiffer rear springs (still semi-elliptic) with rising rate—and the big news, a completely new ball-joint front suspension.

Designed by Earle MacPherson, a recent recruit from GM, the '52s front suspension eliminated king-pins for the first time in a Lincoln and did away with spindle supports as well. This not only made steering much easier, it improved the tracking of the front wheels, and also made it quicker to lube the front end by eliminating more than half of the grease fittings.

The new engine was a 317.5ci, 90deg V-8, which churned out a moderate 160hp at 3900rpm and a very

All 1954 Lincoln models featured running improvements to the 205hp ohv V-8 engines, improved body structures, and new interior trim fabrics and upholstery. This Cosmopolitan four-door sedan also has wraparound bumpers to give it greater visual length. *Credit: Ford Motor Company*

good 284lb-ft of torque at 1800rpm. Compression, strong for the early 1950s, was 7.5:1, and the engine was slightly oversquare with a 3.80x3.50in bore and stroke. Quieter and smoother than the previous out-of-balance flathead engine, this new motor was the best engine a Lincoln had seen since the Leland V-12.

By 1952, Lincoln engineers had finally figured how to economically produce a hardtop body, and a darn fine hardtop it was. These new Lincolns were thoroughly modern-looking cars with an exciting, dynamic appearance, and the power to justify it. The body shells of these new Lincolns were slightly more compact than their predecessors, but the cars themselves were now squarely aimed at the top segment of the market. They

This 1954 Capri convertible has a different front end with a more massive bumper. It, too, has an improved carbu- retor and distributor under the hood. And is that Shirley Temple behind the wheel? *Credit: Ford Motor Company*

were no longer competitors for Buick and Oldsmobile but were the direct counterparts of Cadillac, Packard, and Imperial. This move back upmarket was a wise choice for Lincoln, because it regained the exclusivity of the brand.

These new vehicles, with their excellent new suspensions, ohv V-8 engines, and updated interiors, received only minor styling changes through the mid-1950s. Their outstanding road manners were conclusively proved in an unlikely venue: racing. They received positive reviews from the majority of the automotive press. Prices continued their upward climb, with the Cosmopolitans ranging from $3,517 for a Custom Four-Door Sedan, to $3,622 for the Custom Sport Coupe. A Capri Special Custom Coupe cost $3,866, and the Capri Special Custom convertible rolled out the door for $4,025.

For 1954, the body-side chevron was changed to a smaller V which led the rear fender skirt and trailed into a chrome strip. The 1955 model year Lincolns were even more different, heading toward the unusual cars they would become by the decade's end. The rear clips of the cars were lengthened and, in the case of the two-door coupes especially, this made them look tail heavy. A new taillight treatment completed a different rear fender line, but the fronts of the cars, from the B-pillar forward, remained mostly the same.

By 1955, the Cosmopolitan name had run its course and was completely eliminated. The entry-level cars were now badged as Customs, with Capris as the top-of-the-line models. Dual exhaust systems were standard equipment in 1955, and air-conditioning became available as well. The Lincoln A/C was a complex affair, with its compressor in the engine compartment

More at home with this year's styling elements than the four-door sedans is the 1954 Capri Special Custom Coupe. These vehicles cost $3,869 and were the biggest selling Lincolns of the year, with 14,003 cars sold. *Credit: Ford Motor Company*

and the rest of the system in the trunk. Cold air was blown into tubes running over the door frames and entered the passenger compartment through vents above the windows.

In 1956, the most exciting news from Lincoln may have been the introduction of the new Continental Mark II, but the Lincoln sedans and coupes were completely new as well. The 1956 bodies marked a sharp departure from the middle-of-the-road '52 to '55 model year styles, and although good looking, they led directly to the grotesqueries of the end of the decade.

The 1956 Capri and its new partner, the Premiere, had better visual balance than the 1955s. They were bigger cars and yet had an element of grace. They were, as the ads liked to say, longer, lower, and wider than what had come before. The Premiere was now the top-of-the-line car, with Capri as the step-in model.

The standard engine was retained for 1956, but was modified for more power in 1956, largely from what had been learned in the Mexican road race. The engine was bored out to a larger displacement (368ci) giving 285hp. Compression was increased to 9.0:1, and torque measured just over 400lb-ft, a domestic record in 1956. Inside, the cars were not radically different

from their predecessors, but they were bigger. Controls and the look of the dashboard remained much as before, but there were some mechanical improvements to make controls operate more easily. A new heater was added, with the addition of a warm air outlet under the front seat. Air conditioning was improved for higher output. A new range of interior and exterior colors, including numerous two-tones, made the '56 Lincolns very stylish. In 1956, Lincoln sold much better than in 1955. The double-nickel Lincolns had recorded only a bit over 27,000 units, but the 1956s literally ran out the door. By the end of the model year, Lincoln dealers had truly moved the metal, selling well over 50,000 cars, of which about 4 percent were Capris and the rest Premieres. A Capri Four-Door Sedan went for $4,212, and the Premiere hardtops cost $4,601; the convertibles $4,747.

Through the decade's end, Lincoln styling would become more radical, as the division chased Cadillac for supremacy in the domestic luxury car field, although sales would slump as the US economy went through some hard times.

For the rest of Ford Motor Company, this was an even more trying time, as the company struggled to

For 1955, the Capri Special Custom Coupe had another new front-end treatment with a less complicated bumper than before. Ford's own automatic transmission, Turbo- Drive, became standard equipment, replacing the GM Hydra-Matic, which had been in use for years. *Credit: Ford Motor Company*

come to terms with the Edsel debacle. From Henry Ford II on down, most everyone (with the notable exception of Robert McNamara) thought the Edsel was a good idea. Yet the whole Edsel experience was an unmitigated disaster, the scale of which has rarely been seen in American business. It is a testament to Ford's overall strength that the Edsel didn't do the company more damage than just front-page embarrassment and loss of capital.

Lincoln was smarting from an experience similar only in timing. The Continental Mark II was a splendid car, but at $9,695, it was simply too expensive and exclusive for the market to support. Sales were far below projections in 1956 and 1957, and the cost of producing the car to such lofty standards of fit and finish were even greater than anticipated. Consequently, the Mark II was discontinued at the end of the 1957 model year.

The 1957 Lincolns had few mechanical changes from the '56 cars, but they underwent a styling transformation that was an unfortunate harbinger of things to come. The front end now had four vertically arranged headlamps, which could operate as quads or upper & lower pairs. The rear grew zoomy tail fins, which proceeded rearward from a false air scoop jutting out from the middle of the rear door—or slightly behind the front door in the coupes. The hardtop roof now dominated the whole line-up, and it was a delightfully slender and stylish roof for the era. This roof line gave the '57 Lincolns an overall grace and lightness, despite their growing size and bulk.

There was something restless and untamed about these new Lincolns, something much less conservative than the decade seemed to justify. Little did the public know that this was the last year of sanity for Lincoln design and that the strangest creations of the 1950s were about to burst upon the scene in the guise of the 1958s.

The 1957 model year Lincolns were between 68 and 224lb heavier than their 1956 counterparts and cost about $600 more on the average. To add upscale choices in this healthy sales climate, four-door landau hardtops were added to both Premiere and Capri model lines.

According to Lincoln's Public Relations Department: "This 1956 Lincoln four-door sedan illustrates the trim grace of Lincoln's 'big new look.' More than 18 1/2 feet long—7 inches longer and 2 1/2 inches lower than the 1955 Lincoln—this roomy sedan will carry six adults in uncrowded comfort." A 285hp engine was mandated by that big new body. *Credit: Ford Motor Company*

The standard 368ci V-8 saw several evolutionary modifications for '57. Both pistons and combustion chambers were redesigned for slightly higher compression (10.0:1) and more efficient burn. Added were a throw-away oil filter with a spin-on connection, a Carter four-barrel carburetor drawing through a paper air filter, centrifugal advance distributor, hardened camshaft, and free-flowing exhaust manifolds.

Since the 1955 model year, Lincoln employed its own automatic transmission and was no longer sold with the GM Hydra-Matic. The Ford unit was known as Turbo-Drive. This three-speed automatic used an air-cooled, triple-element torque converter and planetary gearing. It was based on the Ford-O-Matic transmission but given a much higher torque capacity. For 1957, a type of limited-slip differential called Directed-Power was added to the options list, as were power vent windows, electric door locks, and 6-way power seats.

As the decade of the 1950s rushed to a whirlwind conclusion with the launching of Sputnik and the infamous, cold-war "missile gap," Lincoln automobiles underwent a massive change. The cars grew to unprecedented size. They switched to unibody construction, never before tried in cars this big, and they became, to the eye of this writer, excruciatingly, massively, unforgivably ugly.

Now granted, in the history of art, there have been times when innovators such as El Greco, Dali, or Picasso, reached so far into the future that their contemporaries felt what those fine artists had created was ugly. That is exactly what was said about cubism in its beginnings. Picasso himself once remarked that in order to make something beautiful, you must begin by making something ugly. And so it was with Lincoln. The ethereal, classic, and lasting beauty of the 1961 automobiles was, in part, the result of design decisions and trends begun in 1958, the year of the grotesque.

The 1958 Lincolns were truly large automobiles, not altogether because Lincoln executives wanted them so, but because Cadillac was on a large-equals-luxury binge. The '58s were available under three nameplates: Capri, Premiere, and Continental Mark III. The new

This Capri Custom Coupe, photographed on the Ford Proving Grounds in Dearborn, benefits from good design. It is a massive car, but its flowing, graceful lines make it look smaller and well proportioned. *Credit: Ford Motor Company*

Looking inside this 1956 Premiere, along with the perky model, we see the flat, albeit leather-covered, bench seats in two tones, a large diameter, deep-dish safety steering wheel, a new wraparound windshield—and no sign of seatbelts anywhere. *Credit: Ford Motor Company*

Not much resemblance between a 1957 Continental Mark II and the four-door 1957 Lincoln Landau Hardtop Sedan. Higher compression for the Lincoln engine brought its horsepower to 300, and an improved torque converter made driving easier. But, yes, that Landau is a big car. *Credit: Ford Motor Company*

Continental was little more than a styling variation of the Premiere, but the idea of continuing the Continental name was undoubtedly a good one.

The 1958 Lincolns were a full 228in overall and 80.1in wide. They rode on 131in wheelbases—actually greater than today's minivans! While there was some variation in weight depending on the model and trim, these cars tipped the scales at about 4800lb, although the Continental Mark III convertible actually exceeded 5000lb.

They were powered by a new engine, a 430ci V-8 with 10.5:1 compression. This engine was used in all Lincoln products in 1958, and in some Mercurys and Edsels as well. It produced 375hp at 4800rpm and a massive 490lb-ft of torque at 3100rpm. Although we can't verify the power output of that engine when new, some historians claim that Ford overstated the horsepower of this motor. Whatever its real horsepower number may have been, the torque figure has not been disputed, and it represents the kind of power that these huge, heavy cars really needed: off-the-line acceleration and passing ability. Contemporary test results show these barges posting 0-60 times slightly under nine seconds.

The Capri, Premiere, and Continental were all available in sedan and hardtop body styles, as two- and four-door models. With the obligatory convertible for the Continental.

Styling for these '58s was a case of elements run amok. The rear ends resembled Cadillacs; the front ends resembled Chryslers; the hammerhead rooflines, with their reversed rear windows on the Continentals, resembled something from Mars. The heavy front bumper ended with a spread Y shape that flowed back into the sculptured coves around the front wheel arches. This shape may have been an attempt to recall the famous classic lines of the LeBaron cove, but it simply added another wild element to the car's already mixed bag of variations on a deformed brick. The rear wheels had partial skirts, and the mountainous rear bumper completed several of the body's character lines. Blame John Najjar for the mess; he was the lead stylist for these Lincolns.

Due to the strange looks of these cars and word of mouth that their unibody construction was not quite right, Lincoln sales slipped to just under 30,000, the

The longer, lower, wider madness was in full swing at Lincoln in 1957. But despite a massive front bumper and grille, vertical "Quadra-Lites," and a semirounded tail fin at the rear, this Premiere Hardtop Coupe still exhibits good lines thanks to its thin roof and symmetrical front and rear ends. *Credit: Ford Motor Company*

lowest number in three years. Part of this can be explained by the recession that hit the US economy around that time, but part is certainly due to the public's less than wholehearted acceptance of these new models. Actually, 1958 saw a popular rejection of all such excesses from Detroit.

The Mark III also featured a distinctive front and rear grille of similar mesh material to the Mark II. It also had six taillights where the other Lincolns had two, and the four-pointed Lincoln star was featured on the rear grille and the gas filler door. Exclusive leather hides

from Bridge of Weir in Scotland were used as seat covering material and were color matched to deep pile carpeting, although the interior was still not as plush as that of the Mark II.

The Mark III was available as a two- or four-door sedan, hardtop, landau, and a two-door convertible, with a unique rag top that stowed in the trunk below a hinged rear deck panel. This mechanism was inherited from the Ford Skyliner convertible of 1957. The convertible was a very heavy car, due to the extra weight of the top mechanism and various body stiffening cross-

Gone are the sleek lines of 1956 and '57. Some people called this design of John Najjar's the "pagoda," because it had so many mixed elements and ornaments. The dual headlamps are now angled, the front and rear of the car are blocky and massive, and it is bigger than ever. *Credit: Ford Motor Company*

The Premiere Two-Door Coupe does not have the reverse tilted backlights of the Continental but resembles it in most other ways. *Credit: Ford Motor Company*

beams that were added to the chassis. It weighed in at 5040lb, heaviest of the Lincolns for that year.

The Mark III four-door sedan sold for $6,072, the two-door hardtop for $5,825, the four-door landau for $6,072, and the convertible for $6,283. Continental sales dominated the Lincoln marque for 1958 with 12,550 units, versus 6,859 Capris and 10,275 Premieres. The total of 29,684 was substantially down from the previous year and caused these unattractive vehicles to be mildly restyled for the following year. The four-door Capri had a price of $4,951, and the Premiere Sedan cost $5,565.

For 1959, Lincoln simply continued with the '58 models, and gave them minor styling and mechanical changes to address customer complaints. The front wheel cove was flattened and became less dramatic, the unibody was reinforced at the front end and the cowl for less shake or flex, and prices rose anywhere from

Left, powered by a 375hp engine, the 1958 Continental Mark III convertible actually had some performance. Just don't look for a great 0 to 60 time due to the 5040lb body weight. The Continental Mark III is nothing more than a trim level of the standard Lincoln body. *Credit: Ford Motor Company*

$30 to $700, making many Lincolns more expensive than their Cadillac equivalents. The new '59 Continentals were referred to as Mark IVs, and they showed only minor trim differences from the previous models. The Capri name was dropped for 1959, without replacement.

Engine horsepower sagged slightly due to a reduction in compression, but otherwise the powertrain was the same as in 1958. By now, the Continental Division had been quietly folded back into Lincoln-Mercury-Edsel (usually abbreviated as M-E-L).

Hess & Eisenhardt, the famous coachbuilders and Lincoln modifiers, were enlisted by the factory to provide limousine and Town Car models of the Mark IV Continental. The conversion featured black paint and a padded vinyl roof with a formal rear facia; no rear power windows in these exclusive models. But overall, less than 150 of these specials were sold. A Continental Mark IV limousine was available from the factory in 1959, the first Lincoln to be called that since 1942. It offered a padded vinyl top, a high-gloss black paint scheme (known as Presidential Black), and a plush leather interior. The limousine sold for $10,230, and only forty-nine were produced.

Massive, and with the aerodynamics of a brick, this 1958
Two-Door Hardtop Coupe also has the 375hp engine and
unibody construction. *Credit: Ford Motor Company*

Sales numbers dropped again in model year '59 with 11,126 Continentals sold, 7,851 Premieres, and 7,929 Lincolns—the Capri having been discontinued. At 26,906 units, this was the lowest number since 1948. Clearly, changes were needed. But radical change wouldn't be coming at the beginning of the new decade, the turbulent 1960s. Lincoln was not ready with an all-new model, although it had one in the wings. Sales dipped again to a new low for the decade: 11,806 Continentals, and 13,734 other Lincolns.

For 1960, Lincoln proceeded on another variation of the '58 design and platform. The Continental was now known as a Lincoln Continental and was called the Mark V. The chassis returned to Hotchkiss drive and rear leaf springs, instead of the coils that had been used in '58 and '59. The engine continued along the same lines, but now with a two-barrel carburetor for better fuel economy. Sound-deadening insulation was added to the body, and the interior received a slight makeover. These Band-Aid fixes did little to endear the 1960 Lincolns to the public. The division saw another

bad year of sales, with the numbers slipping to 24,820.

It was widely felt that Lincoln had to get a grip and produce an outstanding car or else it might not survive. Lincoln executives knew only too well how severely Ford had acted to eliminate the Edsel when it did not perform up to expectations.

While you may think my comments and stance on the late 1950s Lincolns to be harsh, keep in mind that these ungainly cars with their lack of genuine quality control surrendered more than half of Lincoln's hard-won market share to the competition, mostly Cadillac. Sales had gone from 50,322 in 1956 to a meager 24,820 units in 1960. Lincoln was on the skids.

Fortunately, the division's savior, the 1961 Lincoln Continental, a superb car and a modern classic, was just heading into production. It would not only turn the fortunes of the division around, it would become one of the most sought-after cars in modern history. As before in its often bumpy past, when Lincoln needed a miracle, it got one.

Left, although many details were changed for 1959, the Lincoln body remained mostly the same—ugly. Changes included bringing the styling cove into the front door, a chrome spear and appliqué at the rear quarter, and a new wraparound bumper and grille. *Credit: Ford Motor Company*

The Continental Mark IV retained the reversed backlight for 1959 but shared most of the other styling changes with the other Lincolns. *Credit: Ford Motor Company*

Left, possessing a much better profile than in recent years, the 1960 Lincoln Landau now has a greenhouse that better balances the lower part of the car. Many of the wild lines of the 1958 have been subdued, and styling seems ready for a new direction. *Credit: Ford Motor Company*

A completely new instrument panel was featured in the 1960 Lincoln Continental. Power steering, power brakes, automatic transmission, padded instrument panel, and padded visors were all standard equipment. The model is trying to tell us that she would be very impressed with any man who drove a Lincoln. *Credit: Ford Motor Company*

These two pages, it's still a barge, but the 1960 Continental is the best looking of this large and square style of Lincoln at the turn of the decade. This vehicle had a new Hotchkiss rear suspension with leaf springs and a new, more luxurious interior. *Credit: Ford Motor Company*

Chapter 3

The Marks—Personal Luxury and Performance From the Continental Mark II Through the Spectacular Mark VIII

One notion essential to Lincoln's success in the modern era is the idea of "personal" luxury vehicles. Based on a European concept, personal luxury implies a strong performing two-door coupe or convertible with a lavish complement of comfort and or luxury items. It's what the Europeans themselves would call a "Grand Touring" car. This idea entered the Lincoln universe with the original Continental, based in large part on Edsel Ford's admiration for European cars such as Bentleys, Bugattis, Mercedes-Benz, and other luxury roadsters of the 1920s and '30s.

Since the debut of the original Continental, Lincoln has often investigated the concept of personal luxury, sometimes with great success, sometimes with a resounding thunk. For the most part, Lincoln has led the way in this genre, using both the idea and the reality of the original Continental to point toward new vehicles. It is one of the few categories in which Lincoln has consistently dominated its arch rival, Cadillac—although not every Lincoln Continental "Mark" has been a true personal luxury car, nor true to the original Continental concept.

On October 6th, 1954, William Clay Ford stunned and delighted a group of original Lincoln Continental owners, who had gathered in Dearborn to rally and display their cars, with the announcement that Ford had created a Continental Division and that a brand-new Continental was in the final planning stages even then. Edsel Ford's youngest son smiled as he mentioned that since 1948, when Lincoln discontinued the original Continental, Ford Motor Company received many inquiries about when a new Continental might be available. Now his answer was—soon! The new Continental would appear as a 1956 model.

As word spread about the new car, speculation ran wild both inside Ford Motor Company and in the press. *Motor Trend* and other car-buff magazines ran themselves ragged trying to keep up with a torrent of disguised prototypes and cunning misinformation from Ford. Actually, plans for the reborn Continental had begun in July 1952 when William Clay Ford took command of a Special Projects Division, a thinly disguised ruse to hide the creation of the new Continental.

The first order of business for this new division was to determine what made the original Continental so special, so unique. What was it that generated all the interest in the car Bob Gregorie built for Edsel Ford? After much debate, W.C. Ford and his team were able to put their brief on paper.

They wrote that: "The original Continental filled a gap in the passenger car market by offering a vehicle whose beauty lay primarily in its honesty and simplicity of line." Using that stiff but adequate definition as a starting point, the group characterized their new Continental as "modern, formal, functional, enduring: emphasizing an air of distinction and elegant simplicity."

However, the major hurdle in this process was not defining the new Continental but designing it! After all, Bob Gregorie, creator of the original Continental, was no longer with the company. He had retired for the second time in 1948, after his designs for the 1949 Fords were rejected in favor of independent work done by George Walker.

At any rate, Lincoln did not have Gregorie's genius to tap when planning the new Continental. Of course, that doesn't mean the division was strapped for design or

HISTORY OF THE CLASSIC LINCOLN CONTINENTAL LOOK

1939

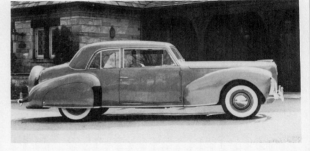

1940

1956

1963

The clean, low classic lines of the original Lincoln Continental (upper left) have been carried right through to the current model (lower right). Conceived in 1939 by the late Edsel Ford as his custom-built personal car, the Continental became a limited production model in 1940 (upper right), when the much-copied "hooded" steel-top version was introduced. From 1939 to 1948, some 5,000 were built. After a lapse of seven years, the Continental was revived in the $10,000 modern classic Mark II (lower left). Only 3,000 Mark II Continentals were built from 1955 to 1957. Current Lincoln Continentals, retaining distinctive styling continuity from early Continentals and the Mark II, have been accorded awards and recognition throughout the world for design excellence.

engineering talent. Its head designer was now John Reinhart, a capable and experienced stylist. Reinhart began his design career with GM and contributed to the interior of the Cadillac 60 Special, the design that set Bill Mitchell on the fast track at GM. Reinhart then worked with Gordon Buehrig, the man who designed the classic coffin-nosed Cords. Reinhart also served a stint at Packard and Studebaker, then joined Ford in 1951.

Working with a design team that included Robert Thomas and Ray Smith, Reinhart first took an evolutionary approach to the new car. He started with the last year of the original Continental, 1948, and attempted to bring the car up to date by drafting a series of new models, just as though the car had stayed in production all along.

Unfortunately, when Henry Ford II saw the results of this design study, he could hardly conceal his contempt. Another solution had to be found. William Clay Ford solicited several other designers to submit proposals for the new Continental, and the in-house department also experimented with some new looks for the car. All these studies were reviewed by Henry Ford II and the executive committee. When they had picked their favorite, Dearborn celebrated; it was one of the designs drawn by Reinhart and the home team.

The new Continental, known as the Mark II, was a beautiful, classy automobile. Appearing at a time when American car design was declining into chrome gimmicks, gewgaws, fins, flares, and frippery, the Mark II set a new standard for restraint and classic simplicity.

Distinctive and elegant, the new Mark II Continental cap-
tures much of the jaunty lines of the original. Notice just
how low the front end of this car is. Very daring for the
time. This 1957 Continental is virtually identical to cars
from the first year of production—1956. *Credit: Ford
Motor Company*

Inside, the new Continental Mark II has a well-planned interior with many elegant touches. The hood over the instrument cluster and the rest of the dashboard are covered in leather, dyed to match the interior colors. Leather-covered seats are standard, as is thick pile carpeting. A tachometer is included with the instruments, but it is relegated to the far right side of the instrument panel. *Credit: Ford Motor Company*

Clearly one of the outstanding designs of its era, the 1957 Mark II still looks good decades later thanks to its simplicity of line and understated decoration. Contrast this car with the Continental Mark III a year later. *Credit: Ford Motor Company*

Suddenly the good looks have fled and been replaced by the shoe box from Hell. The 1958 Continental Mark III was one of those cars that you later regret—and that's exactly what Lincoln did. Later, they recycled this name for the outstanding Mark III of 1968. *Credit: Ford Motor Company*

It's no strain on credibility to say that the Mark II was among the best-looking American cars of the decade; it simply was.

Huge pains were taken to ensure that the Mark II was without peer among domestic personal luxury cars. For example, Mark II engines were dynamometer tested and then broken down for inspection before being mounted in their chassis. Bolts were aircraft grade and were torqued to aircraft specifications. Wheel and tire assemblies were precision balanced by hand.

Transmissions were road tested for smoothness before they were installed in a finished car. All body panels were painted in a special rig, receiving simultaneous coats of paint for superior color matching. The upholstery was trimmed from a single bolt of cloth per car or covered in world-class Bridge of Weir leather hides, which were triple inspected for quality and color. Each individual car was shipped to the receiving dealer in a canvas cover with fleece lining, just like the Lincolns of old. The public premiere of the Mark II took place at the Salon des Automobiles in Paris in October 1955. The response was rapturous.

The Mark II was a completely new vehicle that shared few parts with the rest of the Lincoln line. It used the "cow belly" type frame (favored by body engi-neer Gordon Buehrig and chief project engineer Harley Copp), which had frame rails that bulged outward along the passenger compartment (and led to its farm-yard nickname). This frame allowed the seats to be dropped several inches lower than in an X-braced frame, which made for a lower silhouette and a much lower center of gravity.

The new Mark had a 126in wheelbase and extend-ed for 218.5in overall. It weighed between 4900 to 5000lb and had the 368ci V-8 making 285bhp. Engine output was increased to 300bhp in 1957 through a boost in compression. The lowness of the body dictat-ed that the desired twin-exhaust system would detour around the outside of the frame.

Although the drivetrain was standard Lincoln, with the extra care and inspections added, the chassis fea-tured a triple-jointed drive shaft. One radical, futuristic chassis item was adaptive front suspension. The front shock absorbers used heat-sensing springs internally which stiffened up as the car speeded up or was driven more aggressively.

Indeed there was only one problem with the Mark II: price. At $9,695, it was the most expensive 1956 car in the United States. Not that it wasn't a fine automo-bile but, in retrospect, it is clear that Ford and the Lin-

In 1959, the Mark IV was again little more than the standard Lincoln body with the forward tilted backlight. However, in '59, a distinctive stainless steel bracket framed the unusual angle of the rear window. It curves up around the roofline and descends on the other side—like a decorative roll bar. *Credit: Ford Motor Company*

coln-Mercury Division both vastly overestimated the number of Americans who could comfortably pay that amount for an admittedly "personal" car. With Cadillacs, Buicks, and other Lincolns selling in the $5,000 to $7,000 range, the Continental was simply priced too far above the ceiling established by the market.

It's understandable that Lincoln wanted a car that defined the top end of the domestic automobile, what today is called the "halo" effect and typified by cars like the Mark VIII and the Chevrolet Corvette ZR-1. Sadly, the Mark II was simply too far ahead of its time, always a deadly sin in the car business.

At first, however, sales of the revived Continental were lively, and wealthy buyers couldn't get enough of the car. But quite soon the market exhausted itself, and dealers began to panic. Those who had been selling the car above sticker dropped to the suggested price; some actually began discounting. Overall, between 2,400 and 2,500 Mark IIs were built for 1956 and a scant 444 for 1957, not counting prototypes. On May 8, 1957, the Continental Mark II was officially dropped from the Lincoln product line, but it had already been moribund for several months. On a note of supreme irony, the Oakwood Boulevard plant where the exquisite Mark had been made was refitted to produce a new Lincoln-Mercury product, the Edsel!

One fascinating piece of Lincoln lore concerns the existence of Continental Mark II convertibles. Known to be part of the product strategy from the onset, the production convertibles never made it to the street due to the cancellation of the product line in 1957. At least one factory convertible Mark II was made for Mrs. William Clay Ford. This one-off, painted a light blue, was updated from 1956 to '57 specifications, and had an elegant blue-and-white interior with plush black carpeting. The convertible conversion was performed by Derham Customs of Rosemont, Pennsylvania. But, the plot thickens.

At least one and possibly two Mark II owners are believed to have commissioned and received ragtop conversions of their own, although the whereabouts of these cars today is not widely known, if at all. Today, a convertible Mark II Continental would be one of the rarest and most prized of any American collectible car.

However difficult the experience with the Mark II may have been for Lincoln, the public's strong response

Like a big, grown-up Thunderbird, the 1968 Mark III has classic lines and a sporty character. It was instantly popular. We have Lee Iacocca to thank for bringing back the Marks. *Credit: Ford Motor Company*

to the Continental brand was not lost on the division. For 1958, the Continental name continued with a new car known as the Mark III. Unlike the Mark II, this vehicle was nothing more than a Lincoln Premiere with some styling tricks. The Mark III shared the 430ci engine with the other Lincolns and featured the same unibody construction. It also featured the same ungainly body as the other '58s. However, the Mark III was given its own cross to bear in the form of a rear-tilted rear window with a large center panel that raised and lowered under power—the unfortunate double of the Mercury Turnpike Cruiser.

Because of the power in the Continental name, even the wonderful post-1960 Lincolns would be called Continentals, although they were clearly in the sedan mode (convertibles excepted) and not adherents of the "personal luxury" concept which the Continental name was meant to signify. Indeed, Lincoln devotees would have to wait until 1968 before the Continental Mark line advanced another true knight.

Lee Iacocca was still a rising star at Ford World Headquarters in the late 1960s, and he personally ramrodded the creation of a new Lincoln Mark through its gestation process. Supervised by Iacocca and veteran designer Eugene Bordinat, the new Continental Mark was called the Mark III, partly to wipe the slate clean of the pseudo Marks of the late 1950s, and to give that august name a chance for a new start.

Always striving for economy, Iacocca pulled the same sleight of hand with the new Mark that he used so successfully inderiving the Mustang from the Falcon. The Mark III was founded on the post-1966 four-door Thunderbird platform and body shell, but with extensive reworking of sheet metal and interior fitments.

In fact, the origin of the car is supposed to have been a late-night call from Lee Iacocca to Gene Bordinat saying, "...take the Thunderbird and put a Rolls Royce grille on it!"

This Continental Coupe shows how much difference the little things can make. Also a 1968 model, it does not have the aggressive lines or pure classical revival of the Mark III.

The second Mark III was a handsome car, with classic long-hood, short-deck proportions. It featured a superb mixture of "blade-side" motif from the existing Continental with a bold neoclassic radiator shell and spare-tire bump on the trunk lid. This new Mark also had hidden headlights (shades of 1949), which contributed to its elegantly simple face. Boldly angular, yet not awkward, the Mark III was a departure for Lincoln and would start a new bloodline that continues, in essence, with the Mark VIII of the mid-1990s.

Arriving in April 1968 but promoted as a '69 model, the Mark III of 1968 rode on a 117.2in wheelbase and had an overall length of 216.1in. It was 79.4in wide and 52.9in tall. Both front and rear track were 62in. The Mark III was a rear-drive automobile, with Lincoln's new 460ci motor rated at 365bhp. The rest of the drivetrain consisted of a Ford C6 automatic transmission and Ford 9-3/8in differential. The Mark III weighed 4739lb and carried the highest Lincoln base price tag of that year at $6,585.

It was big and square, but the new Mark III had an undeniable grace and harmony of design. The classical statement of the hood and grille blends perfectly with the dynamics of the bladed fenders and sculpted slab sides. What a fine-looking machine. *Credit: Ford Motor Company*

While not everyone loved the car from the start, it was clear that the new Mark was a success. Sales for the first model year of production totaled 7,770, with a stunning increase to 23,088 for 1969. This vehicle proved so popular that it became the next best thing to happen to Lincoln in the decade of the 1960s after the superb 1961 Continental sedan. It underwent only minor changes until 1972, when a revised version met public scrutiny under the name Mark IV.

Although the Mark IV bore a slight resemblance to the Olds Toronado (around the front bumper and front fender blades) it was a smoother, sleeker car than the

Mark III. A true hardtop coupe, it had a 120.4in wheelbase within an overall length of 220.1in. It was also wider than the previous Mark by 1/2in and offered more interior room. It was slightly lighter in weight than the Mark III, but cost a bit more at $8,640.

One notable feature of the new Mark was its available oval opera window in the rear quarter panel of the roof. This modest styling touch began a trend in the '70s that saw any car with pretensions of class sporting a small window pane in its sail panel. Kits appeared on the aftermarket to put oval windows where they were never meant to go, such was the popularity and influence of the new Mark line.

Sales reflected this newfound stardom for the Mark IV. For 1972, it sold a claimed 48,591 cars, a new record, and a number in excess of Continental sales for the same year.

There was only one fly in the ointment for the Mark IV, and another item of Lincoln lore. The interior for the new Mark was much more like that of the Thunderbird than that of the Mark III. In fact, there are stories of Marks arriving at dealerships with T-Bird logos on the dash, and T-Birds whose dashes proclaimed them to be Mark IVs a substantial embarrassment for the Lincoln dealer, and all due to some sloppy quality control at the plant!

Despite such gaffes, the Mark line continued in unprecedented popularity. Still powered by the 460ci V-8 engine, the Mark IV sold just under 70,000 units for 1973. But the 1973 cars were spoiled somewhat by new government regulations. The front end lost part of its classic look due to the addition of hardware to meet a 5mph bumper rule, and the engine dropped 4hp (to 208 SAE net) due to increasing smog regulations, as yet unredeemed by the advent of fuel injection and electronic engine management. Electronic ignition did appear as an addition to the Mark IV in the spring of '73.

Beginning a trend that would expand significantly in the following years, the Mark IV offered a special trim and decor package known as the Silver Luxury Group. This package consisted of silver paint and a sil-

When Lee Iacocca asked for a "Rolls-Royce" radiator on the Mark III, he got what he wanted. Bold and elegant, this design is instantly recognizable as a Lincoln automobile. Such high impact styling helped establish the Continental Marks as leading "personal luxury" cars from Lincoln. *Credit: Ford Motor Company*

With a profile that instantly recalls the Continental Mark II from the late 1950s, the Mark III has grace and style. It also adds a touch of power and performance with its wheel covers that reference a large octagonal nut at the center, a racing type design. *Credit: Ford Motor Company*

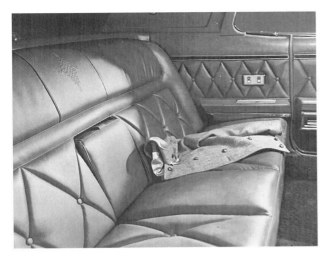

Using a button and tuft style of upholstery, the rear seat of the Mark III was still large enough for adults to feel comfortable. The fold-down center armrest was standard equipment and a favorite place for losing coins, combs, and other flat objects. *Credit: Ford Motor Company*

ver vinyl top, silver leather interior, and a special moon roof with an external silvered coating that turned it into a one-way mirror.

For 1974, the Marks remained much the same, except for even less attractive front and rear bumpers, and newly offered decor packages. The Silver Luxury Group returned but with some added choices of trim and color. It was joined by a Gold Luxury Group and a Saddle

Credit: Ford Motor Company

A smart-looking car and a sturdy competitor for the Cadillac Eldorado, the Mark III is powered by a 460ci engine that delivers 365hp at 4600rpm. *Credit: Ford Motor Company*

and White model with white exterior and saddle leather interior, by far the most tasteful of the new and slightly tacky decor packages.

Sales sagged slightly in 1974 due to the first of the oil shocks in the 1970s. The results of this socioeconomic shock wave would have an increasing and negative effect on Lincoln and the Continental Marks as the decade wore on. For 1974, the Mark IV sold 57,316 cars at a base price of $10,194, reflecting a weakness in the industry overall.

The 1975 model year saw almost no substantive changes to the Mark IV, and sales once again declined, partly due to concerns over rising gasoline prices and partly due to the increased popularity of the Continental Town Coupe, a two-door version of the Continental sedan that had been introduced in 1974 and which captured some sales from the Mark. The Town Coupe had an Eldorado-like profile and a roomier interior than the Mark.

The proliferation of special decor packages continued with the Lipstick and White Group, and the Blue Diamond Luxury Group. The tasteful years of the 1961 Continental and the '68 Mark III were rapidly fading into history as Lincoln scrambled to make its cars appealing to the nouveau riche of the post-Nixon era.

To counteract slipping sales, 1976, the bicentennial year for the United States, saw the beginning of the "Designer Edition" Lincolns and as well as the transfer of many former standard items into the option column of the window sticker. There were eight basic group packages for 1976, but these could be partly mixed, with a huge number of resulting outcomes. The designer packages consisted of cars with trim groups chosen by leading fashion designers and were supposed to appeal to more style conscious buyers. Named after Cartier, Givenchy, Bill Blass, and Emilio Pucci, these Marks had the designers' own signatures inscribed on the rear opera window and on a gold plated plaque affixed to the dashboard.

Based, in part, on the designers' signature color palettes, the Cartier Edition was an overall dove gray (including velour cloth seats) with red pinstriping; the Givenchy Edition featured a turquoise body with white vinyl top and side moldings, dual black-and-white pinstriping, and a turquoise velour interior...no gagging, please. The Pucci Edition was dark maroon inside and out, with a silver vinyl top, and dual silver-and-red pinstripes. The Bill Blass Edition reclaimed some sanity with a navy blue exterior, off-white top, cream-and-gold pinstripes, and an interior choice of dark blue

Although the Mark IV bears a slight resemblance to the Olds Toronado, it is a smoother, sleeker car than its predecessor. A true hardtop coupe, it has a 120.4in wheelbase within an overall dimension of 220.1in. It is also wider than the previous Mark by a 1/2in and offers more interior room. *Credit: Ford Motor Company*

velour or cream-toned leather.

Remember eight-track tapes? The 1976 Mark IVs carried eight-track players as optional equipment along with their AM/FM multiplex stereo radios, to be enjoyed on a Ford Quadrasonic speaker system. Despite, or perhaps because of, the Luxury Group packages and Designer Editions, Mark IV sales rose substantially, to 56,110 vehicles.

For '77, the Mark V debuted, although it was no more than a redesign of the Mark IV's bodywork. This new Mark looked more like the Continental sedan, and considerably like the Continental Town Coupe, but with a snazzier roofline. Three vertical vent doors appeared on the front fenders of the new Mark, and side marker lights were increased in size. The new body was more squareish than before and lost some of the harmonious proportion that made the previous Marks so special. One real change was the substitution of a "small-block" 400ci motor with only 179bhp for the 460. The 460, rated scarcely higher that year at 208bhp, was now available as an option, except in California, where it couldn't meet air pollution standards.

Three different kinds of velour interior were available on the Mark V, along with leather: Ultravelour, Majestic velour, and Romano velour. Is that enough velour for you? The four Designer Editions returned with some different color choices, and an unusual front-half vinyl roof on the Givenchy Edition.

Once again, sales responded strongly, and the Mark V sold powerfully, chalking up 80,321 vehicles for the model year. The next year, a virtually unchanged Mark V sold 72,602 units at a base price of $12,099, against Continental sales of 88,088.

After the 1979 model year, Lincoln said good-bye to the large, full-sized cars that had been its mainstay for over a decade. Detroit was frantically downsizing all its products to meet changing public tastes and the higher cost of gasoline. The huge freeway cruisers that had defined the postwar American car were now seen as obsolete and a bit obscene. As usual, Lincoln, as part of ultra conservative Ford, was the last of the manufacturers to make the change, so it had the large car field mostly to itself in 1979.

The '79 Mark V offered a very special package called the Collector's Series, due to the vanishing nature of this whole breed of cars. They were given a special trim package, but were mechanically identical to all other non-Mark Lincolns of that year. The Collector's Series cars were all painted in a high-gloss Midnight Blue, with a similarly hued interior. The Mark V Collector's Series was actually based on the Diamond Ju-

By 1980, the Mark IV had become more square and angular. While the two-tone paint helps to lengthen and trim the car, its bulk is not as attractive as earlier models. *Credit: Ford Motor Company*

bilee Edition of the Mark, which had appeared in 1978 to celebrate the seventy-fifth anniversary of Ford Motor Company. Offered in two colors, light Diamond Blue or Jubilee Gold, the Jubilee Editions and their successors, the Collector's Series, were a fitting last hurrah for the big Lincolns.

Production remained surprisingly high, considering the growing national trend toward smaller cars and the continued success of the import models. By the late 1970s, Mercedes-Benz began to make serious inroads to the once exclusive American luxury market. The greater fuel efficiency of the German cars and their

This Bill Blass Edition is the best of the Designer Edition Marks with a navy blue exterior, off-white top, cream-and-gold pinstripes, and an interior choice of dark blue velour or cream-toned leather. Remember eight-track tapes? The

1976 Mark IVs carried eight-track players as optional equipment along with their AM/FM Multiplex stereo radios, to be enjoyed on a Quadrasonic speaker system. *Credit: Ford Motor Company*

available diesel engines were very desirable in 1979, after the second big gas shortage of the decade. Despite this trend, Lincoln sold 75,939 Mark Vs during the model year.

Downsizing became the dominant trend for Lincoln in 1980, and the new Mark VI was a victim of that philosophy. Now almost identical to the Continentals, the new Mark VI, in two- and four-door configurations, had lost its special heritage and was built on the same body design as the other Lincoln models. However, the two-door Mark rode on the shorter Ford/Mercury chassis with a 114.3in wheelbase and a 216.0in overall length.

While these new Marks were lighter and smaller than their predecessors, they were more expensive. The basic two-door Mark VI was priced at $15,424 and its four-door sister at $15,824. The top-of-the-line was now the Signature Series, a new designation for the

same option and trim package that had been known as the Collector's Edition the previous year but available in more colors. These variants were the most expensive FoMoCo products of their time. The two-door Signature cost $20,940 and the four-door $21,309. These cars were powered by Ford's 302 V-8 as their standard engine, with the 351 Windsor available as an option.

As the Reagan era kicked in with a vengeance, interest in conspicuous consumption increased, and personal luxury cars became a new focus for increasing disposable wealth. While the younger age groups, now called "Yuppies," opted for Porsche, BMW, and Mercedes, seniors and middle age parvenus desired a Lincoln parked in their slot at the country club. While the Mark VI didn't give them much to brag about, a special new vehicle soon would.

One of the most exciting cars ever produced by Lincoln appeared for 1984, the new Mark VII. Also

In 1984, Lincoln rewrote the rule book with the aerodynamic, high-performing Mark VII. The Mark VII and Lincoln Sport Coupe (LSC) set a new standard for combining luxury and great driving potential. The Mark VII has the kinds of speed and road holding that made legends of cars like the Blue Train Bentley. *Credit: Ford Motor Company*

based on the yeoman "Fox" platform, as were the Mustang, Thunderbird, and Continental Sedan, the new Mark VII returned to the great tradition of the 1960s Marks and was not a retrimmed Town Car. Available only as a two-door coupe, the new Mark had sleek aerodynamic styling and a cozy, cockpit-style interior. It also had adequate performance from a 140bhp, fuel-injected version of the 5.0ltr V-8 that worked so well in the Fox chassis. One noteworthy drivetrain item in this rear-drive platform was a four-speed automatic transmission built by ZF in Germany.

For a short period of time, a 2.4ltr, inline-6 turbo-diesel engine, sourced from Steyr but designed by BMW, was also offered on the Mark VII, but its woeful performance, clattering idle, and smelly exhaust didn't inspire potential buyers. A minor but costly miscalculation for Lincoln, the program was never a success, although the option was listed through model year 1985.

Almost identical in dimensions to the Continental, the new Mark was a whole different automobile for Lincoln. It had a brash, youthful quality and a distinctly European character, not to mention its unabashed aerodynamics. Some Lincoln traditionalists didn't care for the car, or for its even more aggressive variant, the

For 1986, the already potent Mark VII made even more noise with a jump in horsepower, thanks to sequential multi-port fuel injection. ABS brakes became standard equipment in '86, and the premium Ford JBL audio system was a new option. Note the keyless entry keypad above the driver's door handle, a popular and useful option that could open one or more doors or the trunk in response to the proper numerical codes.

LSC, for Luxury Sport Coupe. Sales started out rather slowly, but as word of mouth caught on, the car became more and more popular.

For its introductory year, the Mark VII was available in standard trim, as the LSC, and in two designer packages, the Bill Blass version and the Versace. Base price for the new Mark was $21,707; the LSC cost $23,706. The Versace and the Bill Blass topped the line at $24,807.

The popularity of the LSC led to a bold move by the Lincoln-Mercury Division. For 1985, the LSC received the engine that was destined for it all along, the 302 High Output. Rated at 165hp, the HO gave the LSC bravura performance and elevated this machine close to the top ranks of American performance cars of the period. Now Lincoln had something Cadillac simply couldn't match, a car with no lack of luxury and refinement, and with the kind of sweaty-palms performance that was more often associated with the Mustang GT!

To match this elevated performance, antilock brakes (ABS) became standard equipment on the Mark VII for 1985. Lincoln emerged as a leader in safety technology in the 1980s and continues that trend admirably in the 1990s.

Spurred on by enthusiastic reviews in the automotive press and raves from wealthy young owners, the horsepower in the LSC was bumped even higher for 1986, to a potent 200bhp . With this engine package, the Mark VII became a premiere performance machine, the alpha male of its litter, and the Lincoln legend found a new hero. Although the Mark VII did not find a home in motor sports like the 1950s Lincolns that raced in the Carrera Panamericana, they were superb driving machines.

This writer can distinctly remember edging a Mark VII LSC into traffic and burying the gas pedal into plush carpeting. With a roar of power, the LSC laid rubber for a hundred yards while its delighted driver steered the missile past unbelieving faces on the mean streets of Los Angeles.

Next page, sleek and elegant, the Mark VIII is the most radical car Lincoln has ever built, and the most exciting. This 1995 Mark VIII is nearly identical to the initial 1994 model, except for the wheels. The 1994s carry a more traditional Lincoln turbo-fan wheel, as opposed to this twisted five-spoke design. *Credit: Ford Motor Company*

Inside, the Mark VIII continues the metaphor of the "corporate jet" with a wraparound interior that angles the center console toward the driver and gives the passenger surprising room and comfort. *Credit: Ford Motor Company*

By 1988, the LSC had become so popular that the base model of the Mark VII was dropped, and only LSC and Bill Blass versions were available. Prices had increased to $25,016 for either one. For 1989, engine power was again increased, to 225bhp, and performance again took a step forward. Pricing also took a step forward, with the LSC and Bill Blass models both stickered at $27,218.

The LSC, with its muscular grace, its big tires, and powerful engine package was like a return to the great performance coupes of the 1930s: the Blue Train Bentley and the Bugatti Atlantique. Never in its history had Lincoln offered a car with such road ability and such a delightful combination of style and exhilaration.

An even more amazing Lincoln was on the drawing boards by then. Spurred on by the tremendous popularity of the Mark VII, whose sales jumped from 18,355 for 1985 to 38,259 for 1988, Lincoln's product planners, designers, and engineers had plans to push the envelope further still—to limits befitting a car that would likely see the twenty-first century: the phenomenal Mark VIII!

Lincoln truly had taken a risk and been successful with the Mark VII. When it came time to replace that very special vehicle in the early 1990s, Lincoln took an even bigger risk by several orders of magnitude. However, success always requires risks. In the case of the Mark VIII, it is too early to tell what the ultimate acceptance of the car will be. Sales for the first year have been below projections, but they were for the Mark VII also, and that car went on to have a respectable performance on the ledger books. Model year 1993 production of the Mark VIII was 32,370; model year 1994, 28,164.

The Mark VIII is designed to compete with the Cadillac Eldorado, the Lexus SC400, the Acura Legend Coupe, and the Mercedes-Benz E-class cars. Potential buyers have a median age of fifty-six years and average about $100,000 of yearly income. Slightly more than half of them have a college education, and about three-quarters are men. The Mark VIII has definitely moved upscale from the Mark VII.

Built on a unibody platform, the Mark VIII is 207.3in long and uses a 113.0in wheelbase to achieve a very smooth ride. It measures 74.6in wide and stands 53.6in tall. Curb weight is 3768lb. It is meant to seat five, but four would be more comfortable. The powertrain layout is front engine/rear drive, for the best in performance and control. Optional computerized Traction Assist uses elements of the ABS system to eliminate rear

wheel spin and improve handling on wet or snowy roads.

Suspension is the most advanced of any ever used on a Lincoln automobile. In front, unequal length A arms contribute to excellent wheel control and light steering. At the rear, a fully independent arrangement of upper and lower control arms compliments the performance suspension at the front. Both ends have stabilizer or antiroll bars, and both ends use nitrogen gas-pressurized shock absorbers, an element adopted from European performance cars. The truly exotic component of the Mark VIII's suspension is found in the computer-controlled air springs at all four corners. Based on air-spring technology used in the Mark VII and the 1988-94 Continental Sedan, this system uses a computer to govern ride characteristics and has a leveling feature that balances the car fore and aft and from side to side. The system also includes a speed-lowering feature that drops the car by several centimeters at speeds above 40mph to improve aerodynamics and increase fuel economy.

The new Mark takes power from an amazing engine, an all-aluminum 4.6L dohc thirty-two-valve V-8. Based on an advanced family of "modular" engines, the 4.6 dohc produces 280bhp at 5500rpm and 285lb-ft of torque at 4500rpm. These figures, while official, seem quite modest once you've experienced the performance of the car. With all that power on tap, the Mark still delivers a factory-estimated 18mpg in the city and 25mpg on the highway.

Speed-sensitive power rack-and-pinion steering makes the Mark VIII easy to control, as do its 16x7in wheels and P225/60R16 97V BSW tires. The Mark comes to a halt using four-wheel disc brakes, 11.5in in front and 10in at the rear, with standard ABS.

Inside, the driver and passenger luxuriate in a close-coupled, cockpit-style cabin, with a center console that twists toward the driver like a great beast obeying his will. An all-leather interior is augmented by some large stretches of plastic, but wood trim was added for 1994, and that makes for a warmer interior. On the dash, a digital message center displays trip information and various mechanical warnings, including an oil change reminder.

Climate control is fully automatic, set by temperature. The blower uses a "ramp-up" function to keep from blasting hot or cold air into the cabin. Air conditioning is environmentally friendly with R134A refrigerant, free of CFCs. A moonroof is optional, one of a very short list of options. The keyless entry system unlocks the doors, and, from 1994, it disarms the alarm

With its air suspension and notorious ride-height control, the Mark VIII slices through the air like a knife blade. Excellent handling and thunderous power combine with luxury to make this car an outstanding personal vehicle. *Credit: Ford Motor Company*

and positions the driver's seat, steering wheel, and outside mirrors into the driver's preferred positions, although a memory function can readjust the system to suit a second driver.

Dual airbags are standard equipment, along with six-way adjustable power seats, and the power seats have a separate "Autoglide" feature that moves them forward or back when the seatback is tilted forward, to make accessing the rear seats easier.

The Mark VIII has one of the best warranties in the United States with four-year/50,000-mile bumper-to-bumper protection, six-year/100,000-mile corrosion protection, and a two-year/24,000-mile plan for emissions related hardware. Roadside assistance is also part

Distinctive alloy wheels and careful use of chrome trim help add a sporty character to the elegance of the 1994 Mark VIII. *Credit G. Von Dare*

of the overall warrantee package, although in the 1990s it's available on many makes and models.

A smashing car, yes. On paper, the Mark VIII shapes up as one of the most exciting domestic cars ever produced. But what is it like to get behind the wheel of this sleek and stylish machine? Thanks to a week-long test drive, we were able to find out.

If the Mark VIII is an indication of where the concept of personal luxury and performance is headed in the next century, we feel confident that Lincoln is bound for even greater achievements.

ELEGANCE AND EXCITEMENT

Driving Impression: Continental Mark VIII

*I*f you're ready for a life of soothing luxury and stirring performance combined, the Mark VIII may be the choice for you. Representing a quantum step forward in design and engineering, the VIII is not only one of the newest Lincolns, it is arguably the most advanced car the division has ever produced. During a week of driving a jet black Mark VIII with saddle leather interior, we came to appreciate this elegant and roadworthy car for what it is, a corporate jet for the streets.

The Mark VIII feels like what it is, a successor to the LSC. Using the same chassis balance and rear-wheel drive layout, the Mark VIII has the savor of a sport coupe as well as the civilized, luxurious qualities of a touring car. Suspension tuning is decidedly sporty, with a good deal of road feel coming in through the chassis. Steering, however, is not on a par with the more aggressive cars in this class, such as the Lexus SC300/400 or the Mercedes SL500. Still, the power steering has excellent response and crisp turn-in. There is also a noticeable on-center feel to the steering, but it is subtle and makes for a good reference point in compound turns when you need to return the car to a balanced posture before cranking the wheel in the opposite direction for the next turn.

In all, the Mark VIII was a more in-control car than its predecessor, but it still retains some of the ponderous feelings of recent sporty Thunderbirds. Granted, this is not meant to be a fire-breathing sports car with turn-on-a-dime handling. It's a luxurious touring car, after all, and meant to be driven as one. Go too fast, get too aggressive, and the Mark VIII eventually becomes unsettled. A hint about the upper limits of performance can be taken from the excellent leather-covered front seats. They are well shaped and provide enough back support for the average adult, but they have little side bolstering. If you go too fast around yonder curve, the car will give you a signal by making you slide around on the front seat. I know, because I went too fast. Not too fast for the suspension or the chassis or the tires, but too fast for the interior. And that's clearly just too fast.

Every great car is built around a great engine, and that's certainly true for the Mark VIII. The 4.6ltr twin-cam modular V-8 is a delight of an engine and a perfect match for this platform. It provides strong power from a stop, quite a kick in the midrange, and quiet cruising at highway speeds. The thirty-two-valve valve engine has wonderful throttle response, as well as a fine sense of linkage between throttle position and overall speed. If ever the term "hot-rod Lincoln" applied to a car, it has to be this sleek beauty.

Inside, the VIII's cabin is spacious and open. It feels larger than it is. Materials used inside are all first rate, although there is quite a bit of plastic everywhere, an inescapable element today, even in a luxury car. The leather seats are comfortable and broad, easily adjustable with Mercedes-style miniature seat-shaped controls located on the door side of the seat cushion.

The dashboard features large, easy-to-read analog instruments, and a sweep-around style that integrates the dash and the door covers into one unified design. Again, the metaphor of the corporate jet comes to mind. Although it is strange that after angling the center console toward the driver, a row of warning lights at the top of that console should be straight on!

Few cars on the market offer such elevated levels of performance and such deep luxury, combined with such an impressive high-tech array of features. Overall, the Mark VIII is an outstanding driver's car and a vehicle in which it would be effortless to feel pride of ownership.

Although the Continental trunk bulge is low and subtle in the Mark VIII, it identifies the car at once. Lincoln stylists also swear that it functions as a lip spoiler at higher speeds! *Credit G. Von Dare*

Next page, a grille made of a durable but flexible material makes it possible for the Mark VIII to suffer the slings and arrows of parking lot life and still come out looking good. This 1994 Mark VIII shows the high quality of the paint work and the overall superior fit and finish of the car. *Credit G. Von Dare*

Chapter 4

Continuity and Steady Growth— Lincoln In the 1960s and 1970s

Robert Strange McNamara was on the fast track to success at Ford Motor Company in the decades following World War II. Formerly an economics professor at Harvard, he was one of the original Whiz Kids. Thanks to his brilliant mind and humorless, hard-line attitude about cutting costs, he had steadily climbed through the corporate ranks. His achievement with the compact Falcon and his canny rejection of the Edsel gave him a green light for one of the top executive jobs at Ford's corporate level. By 1958, he was in charge of overall automotive operations.

One day in late August 1958, McNamara was touring the design studios and glanced into the Special Projects room. There he viewed a design study for a new generation Thunderbird. The study was supervised by Elwood P. Engel, an associate of George Walker who had become vice-president of styling at Ford.

What McNamara saw stopped him in his tracks. It was a superb two-door styling concept, loosely based on the Continental Mark II but with more modern, more graceful, more beautiful lines than even the legendary Mark. Although McNamara was laconic in the extreme, he became excited as he walked around this car. By the time McNamara left the styling studio, he knew that he had the answer to Lincoln's problems. This design was not going to be a new Thunderbird, it would

From the foggy depths of Elwood P. Engel's design studio came the stunning 1961 Continental. Smaller, more elegant, simple after several years of excess, this new Continental became one of the most influential cars of the decade. That John Kennedy was shot in a Continental put this car's stamp forever on the 1960s. *Credit: Ford Motor Company*

The Continental four-door convertible was the only four-door convertible sold in the United States at that time. The distinctive rear-opening rear doors are another Lincoln trademark. *Credit: Ford Motor Company*

be the 1961 Lincoln Continental! McNamara gave the stylists just two weeks to prepare the concept as a four-door Lincoln. Amazingly, they did it, and the new Lincoln Continental went into production in almost exactly that form.

Even in Lincoln's long and distinguished history, few cars have had the impact of the '61 Continental. Although McNamara was far more of a numbers man than a "car guy," his instinct in this case proved to be remarkable. The new Lincoln Continental offered the best styling to come out of Detroit in a decade, surpassing even the good looks of the Mark II, which served as its inspiration.

Styling of the new Continental was based on a blade-side concept. One long vertical surface formed each side of the car, dominating its profile. Each of these blades had a slight cylindrical bulge. There was no sculpting of the sides except for a slight flare around each wheel well. The fenders ran higher than the decks of the car and created a bladelike line from the front bumper to the taillight. This line was crested with a thin chrome strip in all versions and colors of the vehicle. A slight kick-up in the center of the rear door recalled the beltline of the Mark II while the greenhouse used Ford's modern roofline and added a striking tumble-home or "pagoda" effect as the sides narrowed toward the top.

The four doors latched at the B-pillar and opened out from the middle, a reminder of grander Lincolns from times gone by. The public and press liked to call them "suicide doors," a name coined during the heady days of the 1930s. However, there is no record of anyone purposely ending his or her life by means of the rear doors on a '61 Continental.

Symmetry was another styling hallmark of this car. The front and back facias looked remarkably similar, although each had distinct features. These elegant and understated 1961 Continentals were sold in only two body styles, and they now represented Lincoln's entire line-up. There was a four-door sedan and a four-door convertible—the only four-door ragtop on the American market at the time and the first since the '51 Frazer.

But the new Continental, gorgeous and elegant though it was, also represented a deeper commitment to quality by the Lincoln-Mercury Division than had existed in the recent past. While it was not to be a Mark II with its overwhelming quality controls and delivery procedures, the new Continental still saw a level of preparation that elevated it into a class different from other Ford or Mercury products.

Not only had much more engineering time gone into such items as better sound-deadening for the new Continental's unibody and superior rust proofing, but

Lincoln designers and executives had the good sense to leave the Continental alone for 1962, although there were some detail changes regarding grille, headlights, and bumpers. *Credit: Ford Motor Company*

The interior of a 1962 Continental convertible shows how simple the dash and front seat are. The air conditioner is in that drawer below the radio. It swings down and out for cool air. *Credit: Ford Motor Company*

each car was stringently tested both at the component level and as a completed vehicle. Every one of the Continental engines was subjected to severe examination that included a three-hour burn-in or hot run. Then the engine was stripped down, checked for wear or scuff, and reassembled for final installation. Every electrical part was thoroughly tested by a specialized machine, and rejected if it didn't meet high standards. Convertibles and sedans were given a three-minute bath in a water spray room that duplicated heavy rain conditions, to check for sealing leaks around the win-

dows and doors. A fluorescent dye was added to the oil supply so that any small oil leaks would turn up when the underside of the car was scanned by a black light near the end of the assembly line. For the early 1960s, this was quite innovative.

When the cars were completed, they were road tested at length on a route that took them over a test track at the Wixom, Michigan, plant, and also out onto public roads, where they were driven under a variety of conditions. Lincoln employed sixteen test drivers just for this program. Each car underwent nearly two hun-

The biggest change to the 1962 Continental came at the front end where the 1961's Thunderbird-like headlights and grille were replaced with a more unique design. *Credit: Ford Motor Company*

This page, both the convertible and sedan versions of the 1963 Continental show only minor changes yet again. The car received better suspension and some engine enhancements. *Credit: Ford Motor Company*

While the 1964 Continental looks like more of the same, this year's cars are 3in longer and have 15 percent more luggage capacity. A new roof gives more headroom in front and rear and is 5.4in wider than last year. *Credit: Ford Motor Company*

The convertible shares the changes for 1964, including a new roofline. Notice the new grille and the slight change of shape in the end guards of the bumpers. *Credit: Ford Motor Company*

dred checks before being released for shipping.

Eugene Bordinat, head of the Lincoln Styling Studio, held the opinion that one reason Cadillac had an advantage over Lincoln was Cadillac's continuity of style, even through the giddy, gaudy years of the late 1950s. At the same time, Lincoln had been trying on different looks and styles like a man buying a suit; one comes off, another goes on. Cadillac had developed a recognizable image that people knew and identified instantly. Lincoln had some design success but had not crafted an iconic look. Without Bordinat intending it, the Elwood P. Engel Continental of 1961 would give Lincoln that franchise for the better part of a highly successful decade.

The new Lincoln was relatively modest in size, especially compared to the barges of 1958-60. It had a 123in wheelbase, and a bumper-to-bumper length of 212.4in. Track was 62.1in and overall width was 78.6in. Height varied from 53.5 to 55.2in, depending on model, and weight was 4927lb for the sedan, 5215lb for the convertible.

Power for these new Continentals came from the continued 430ci V-8 that had been in their predecessors, the big boats of 1960. That engine, with its thoroughly oversquare 4.30x3.70in bore and stroke, still produced a rousing 300bhp.

While you might think that a convertible should be lighter than a sedan, since a steel roof has been replaced with a cloth top, remember that the unibody of the vehicle needs structural reinforcing to cope with the loss of strength and rigidity caused by chopping off the top. Plus, the convertible mechanism uses a number of electric or hydraulic motors and other hardware not found on the sedan, all of which add weight.

Although hopes were high at the Lincoln-Mercury Division for these new cars, no one could know that they would become American icons, and would begin to establish Lincoln as a head-to-head competitor of

By 1966, this Continental has added some sculpturing to its sides but still retains the superb simplicity of the 1961.

This two-door has a personality quite distinctive from the upcoming Mark III in 1968. *Credit: Ford Motor Company*

Cadillac for the first time in the history of the marque. The overwhelming success of these '61 Continentals, even though it took a while to accumulate, is borne out by the ever-increasing sales numbers through the decade, and by the attempts of Chrysler Imperial and, yes, even Cadillac to copy the elegance of the design.

For calendar year 1961, Lincoln sold 33,180 vehicles, the make's best calendar year performance since the graceful Lincolns of 1957. Clearly, someone was doing something right.

The plan for design and model continuity at Lincoln was now in effect. As the decade of the 1960s rumbled on, only minor changes were made to the appearance of these cars.

In 1962, the Continentals lost their '61 T-Bird-inspired headlight insets in the front grille and received suspension enhancements to decrease road noise. The convertible tops were improved and now had a firmer look that more closely resembled the steel roofs of the sedans. Inside, the angle of the steering column was changed slightly to better position the steering wheel. Along with all Ford products, Lincoln switched over from Champion spark plugs to Autolite plugs in 1962.

Continental performance was unaffected. As the public became more aware of the elegant new Continentals, sales rose. For the 1962 model year, sales moved up to 31,061 from the 25,164 of the '61 model year.

The rest of the decade saw a similar pattern. In 1963, the Continentals lost a bit of weight (30lb) and gained $200 dollars in price. Power was improved to 320bhp through the return of a four-barrel carburetor, new pistons, and slightly raised compression. Trunk space grew thanks to a redesigned rear deck lid. Interior space was improved through clever adjusting of existing components. Stainless steel mufflers became standard equipment, as did aluminum brake drums on all models; body corrosion protection was increased. Lehmann-Peterson of Chicago developed an Executive eight-passenger stretched limousine from the '63 Continental that would become the benchmark for American limo services in the 1960s.

Lincoln engineers didn't want to change the appearance of the Continental, but they had intriguing plans for 1964. That year the Continental was stretched 3in in the rear door area, and the trunk floor was lowered several inches. This increased passenger legroom

Although this four-door Continental shows a number of new styling touches, it remains much the same car as the other Continentals of the 1960s. Overall length for this car is 221in—an increase of 5in over the previous model. This car has much more interior room and 2.5cu-ft more trunk space. *Credit: Ford Motor Company*

and cargo room substantially and made it easier to get into and out of the rear seats. Overall interior volume was up from the 1963 due to the use of flat side glass, a cost-cutting change demanded by McNamara before he left to join the JFK administration. Lincoln managers claimed that they were improving the sealing of the side glass, but it was bean counting. Seatbelts became a standard feature midyear.

The next year, 1965, was a carryover year with several minor changes in trim placement, and a few technical improvements such as transistorized ignition. Sales continued to rise to an annual level of 40,180.

Eager to ride this wave of popularity as far as it would go, Lincoln executives and designers made their most extensive changes to the Continental in 1966, but the car that emerged from the process was unmistakably a new Lincoln, and it was clearly a mild evolution of the durable and classic '61 design.

For 1966, the Continental saw a change in the look of the automobile as the pure slab sides gave way to tall sides with a chamfer, or angle, along the top, as though someone had run a big router along the tops of the fenders. This helped to diminish the bulk of the body, which had been growing in small increments for the

last three years. Although the outer panels were changed, the unibody structure below them was the same as before. Front and rear glass was now more steeply raked than before, and side glass was again curved, but mildly so. The hood now showed a more pronounced central raised area known as a "power dome." This carried forward into the grille and defined a matching crest between the quad headlamps.

On the power side, a massive new engine made its debut—a high compression 462ci V-8 with 340hp and 485lb-ft of torque, quite a stump puller. Other technical refinements included a new steering wheel, a revamped interior, and the C6 automatic transmission (advertised as Twin-Range Turbo Drive), a high-torque version of the popular Ford C4 automatic.

Most notable was the return of a two-door Continental in 1966, the first since '60. The coupe was a hardtop design with no B-pillar, but it lacked the just-right proportions of the sedan and convertible. The coupe weighed 4985lb and sold for a suggested $5,485. In all, 15,766 coupes were sold for 1966, an impressive beginning.

The 1967 model year witnessed little change at Lincoln. Seven vertical bars were added to the front

In cooperation with the Allegheny-Ludlum Steel Company, Lincoln produced this Continental convertible with an all stainless steel body in 1966. It makes you wonder if that's where John DeLorean got the idea for his brushed stain-less sports car. This Lincoln was the fifty thousandth car produced in that model year, a record for Lincoln in the 1960s. *Credit: Ford Motor Company*

This 1967 Continental Coupe continues with the policy of minor changes. This year's styling relies on the hood's power bulge, new bumpers, and narrow whitewall tires that were becoming popular. *Credit: Ford Motor Company*

Improvements in the car's interior and safety highlighted the 1967 convertible. New product features include a ventilation system that clears the car of smoke or stale air, a new transmission shift pattern, and dual brake system. *Credit: Ford Motor Company*

grille, and the texture of the rear taillights was changed slightly. The four pointed Lincoln star emblem was relocated to the C-pillar of the roof, from the side of the front fender. On the technical side, a dual braking system was introduced, but it utilized a front/rear split rather than the much safer dual-diagonal systems of the '80s and '90s. The transmission was renamed Select-Shift-Turbo Drive and could now be manually shifted. To allow easier shifting, a standardized automatic shift quadrant arrived with a P-R-N-D-2-1 gear layout. Sales were slow for 1967 after the popular redesign of the 1966 model year. Sadly, for 1968, the convertible was discontinued, killed by the bean counters as being too expensive to produce and not strong enough in sales.

During 1968, Lincoln manufactured its one-millionth automobile, a four-door Continental sedan, at the Wixom, Michigan, plant; but the real news of the year was the introduction of the Mark III, a car that took the classic themes of the Mark II and brought them into the dynamic 1960s. The Mark III became one of the most successful cars in Lincoln's history, ultimately enhancing the popularity of the Continental line as well.

Again, only inconsequential changes were made to the Continentals for 1968. A peaked grille appeared, which was not as attractive as previous versions, Goodyear Polyglas tires became standard equipment, and a Town Car interior option group was added. The Town Car name would be a focal point for Lincoln in the years to come.

For 1970, the Continental underwent its first major redesign since the introduction of the vastly influential 1961. First, the '70 was a body-over-frame vehicle. The unibody concept was gone, partly to make this car more like the other large Fords and Mercurys with which it shared a number of chassis and frame compo-

Next page, in 1971, Lincoln celebrated fifty years as a brand name of American cars. To celebrate, a Gold Anniversary Town Car package was devised. It offered Gold Moondust metallic paint, a black vinyl roof, black leather interior, black nylon headliner, Brazilian rosewood interior fillets, and a gold-plated plaque on the dashboard that was inscribed "Golden Anniversary Continental." *Credit: Ford Motor Company*

This page, based on a Lincoln styling exercise that was reworked by Hollywood customizer George Barris, the original Batmobile is one of the most famous cars of the 1960s. *Credit: George Barris Photo*

nents. Boasting a prominent power bulge in the hood and a dominant central grille section, this new body also bore a greater resemblance to other Ford products than had the Lincolns of the 1960s.

Mechanically, this new vehicle had a retuned front suspension and a new rear suspension with trailing arms and coil springs on a live axle. The entire drivetrain was carried over from the previous year with no changes. Front and rear track was increased on the Continentals for 1971, and steel door beams became standard equipment. A new closed fuel delivery system decreased gasoline evaporation, in line with Federal standards.

While this was an imposing vehicle, difficult economic times and a loss of Lincoln exclusivity—not to mention intramural competition from the Mark III—saw the new Continentals selling in lower numbers than they had the previous model year: 37,695 overall. MSRP prices for 1970 were $6,211 for the sedan and $5,976 for the coupe.

In 1971, Lincoln celebrated fifty years as a brand name. To celebrate, a Gold Anniversary Town Car package was devised. It offered Gold Moondust metallic paint, a black vinyl roof, black leather interior, black nylon headliner, Brazilian rosewood interior fillets, and a gold-plated plaque on the dashboard that was inscribed: "Golden Anniversary Continental." At delivery, the new owners were presented with a set of gold plated keys in an elegant wooden box.

Minor front- and rear-end styling changes also marked Lincoln's fiftieth model year. The Continental coupe and sedan's grille was narrowed to the center section, and the hidden headlights were now behind rotating body-colored panels, with a decorative horizontal bar in the center of the headlamp doors. Michelin radial tires, with a single, thin whitewall stripe on their sidewalls, became the new OEM fitment. Once again, Lincoln was going through an ugly phase, and sales slipped, now at their lowest level since 1963, although Mark III sales were still climbing. No one at Lincoln seemed to get the hint.

After the excitement of the Golden Anniversary in 1971, '72 was a model year with little change to both Continental coupe and sedan. Although a new Town Car package debuted mid-year. This vehicle had Lamont cloth as the standard seat covering material, with leather now optional, and clever "mini-vent" windows which looked like the old "quarter-vent" panes, but lifted and lowered electrically and in sequence with the main windows. These Town Cars came with silver plated keys.

Sales of the 1972 model year Continentals showed healthy growth and advanced about 29 percent, to just below the 50,000 level, but were overshadowed by a phenomenal 79 percent increase in sales of the new Mark IV.

While the 1973 Lincolns looked more like Mercurys than ever before, sales did pick up. Some new, stronger stampings improved structural strength in the roof of the Continentals, and B.F. Goodrich tires were the new factory standard rubber. Exhaust gas recycling (EGR) systems became mandatory by federal law on all models. Due to the popularity of the Town Car package, a Town Coupe joined the model line-up. With the runaway popularity of the new Mark IV, and a rebound in sales for the Continental, Lincoln sold a total of 128,073 vehicles for 1973, a record high since 1949.

While most Americans remember that 1974 was the year of the first oil embargo, for Lincoln this was simply another recession year; no big deal. The trend toward smaller luxury cars had come and gone before, and would come again with the 1975 Seville. There was no reason to think it would be any different now. Still, when you saw those endless lines of cars stretching away from beleaguered gas stations, you knew the writing was on the wall for full-sized automobiles, Lincoln included.

For 1974, the Continental got restyled front and back ends. The front turned out much nicer than before, with a more delicate and elegant grille on the car's prominent nose, a grille composed of thin vertical slats, something close to the "waterfall" style. The Town Coupe was similarly changed. Both models lost those ornamental coverings on the rotating headlamp covers. The face of the Continental was now much easier to look at. 1975 saw a restyle of the sheet metal and a new roofline. The Continental sedan now offered vinyl roofs as standard equipment as well as the notorious oval opera window in the roof's rear quarter. The Town Car name continued as an option group, sporting the exterior B-pillar lamp that was optional on other Continental models. Continental coupes now had a concave rear roof edge and blind rear quarters, with an oddly shaped rear window right behind the door seam. Both

Next page, for 1974, the Continental has a new die-cast grille with vertical bars and a Continental name in script replacing the rectangular appliqué on the headlight doors. This vehicle cost $8,238 and weighed 5361lb. Just under 30,000 of them were produced that year. *Credit: Ford Motor Company*

the coupe and the sedan developed a massive, Cadillac-like look in the mid-1970s, and Lincoln sales were the best they had been since the postwar boom.

For the 1975 model year, catalytic converters became standard equipment on the Lincoln product line, along with all other Ford vehicles. The increased exhaust back-pressure of the converters made an already weak horsepower situation slightly worse. The same physical 460ci V-8 that produced 365hp in a 4719lb car in 1970 was now dribbling out 206 or 194bhp (in California) against a 5229lb body—the days of the storied mid-fifties hot-rod Lincoln were history.

As for prices, a 1975 Continental coupe began at $9,214, a Continental four-door sedan was $9,656, and the Continental Mark IV hardtop coupe set its owner back by $11,082. The steep price and lackluster performance of 1975 models hurt sales of the Mark and dropped them to their lowest point since the beginning of the decade. Continental rebounded to a respectable 54,698 units for the 1975 model year, although big changes were not far off as fallout from oil shortages and shifts in the social climate continued to mount.

By 1976, Lincoln's market share had shown a steady climb from a decade earlier, thanks in most part to the success of the stylish Marks. Overall, Lincoln sales now accounted for 28.2 percent of the luxury car market, up from 19.7 percent.

The big changes rumbling through American society at this time saw expression at mid-model year 1977 in the creation of the Lincoln Versailles, often called Lincoln's response to the Cadillac Seville. The Seville was notorious in Detroit inner circles as a Chevy Nova chassis, powered by an Oldsmobile engine, covered by an elegant and unique body design realized under the master of the craft, Bill Mitchell. Due to its fine proportions and classy, coachwork styling, the humble origins of the Seville were glossed over by the public, and this downsized Cadillac became a big winner in the marketplace.

The Versailles, despite its classy name, would never be a hit. Based on the Mercury Grand Monarch Ghia, with a Continental-style front radiator shell and a Continental-inspired bulge in the trunk lid, the Versailles might be better compared to the later Cadillac Cimarron, which was similarly rejected by the public as a blatant attempt to add superficial trim features and options to a cheap vehicle and market it as a downsized luxury car.

Despite all the ups and downs that Lincoln had suffered through the years, the current Continentals could still trace their heritage back to the glory days of Henry Leland and Edsel Ford. The poor Versailles was significantly lacking in this pedigree.

The Versailles was just under 201in from stem to stern, on a 109.9in wheelbase. Front track measured 59.0in and rear tread was slightly smaller at 57.7in. Overall width exceeded track width by 32 percent; it was 74.0in. Height was an indifferent 54.1in when the car rode on stock forged aluminum wheels and 15in, 78 series tires. It weighed 3200lb and was powered by the Ford corporate 351ci V-8 that delivered an underwhelming 135hp.

Yet, the Versailles did seem like an attempt on Lincoln's part to market a car in keeping with the times—and the times indicated a move to smaller cars, both for their fuel efficiency and to be less ostentatious in an era when bigger no longer seemed to be better. In its introductory model year, the Versailles sold 15,434 vehicles, adding to a record total of 191,355 units for the Lincoln nameplate.

Another minor note for 1977: the Continental was offered with a downsized engine, a 400ci V-8 that developed a meager 179hp. It was available in either the Continental or the Mark V.

Downsizing of engines continued in 1978 when the unlucky Versailles came with only one engine choice, the corporate 302 V-8, dropping two horsepower in the process. Sales of the Versailles plummeted to 8,931, about half of the first year's figure.

The plunging sales figures triggered some kind of ah-ooo-gah alarm in Ford headquarters and, for 1979, the Versailles looked like it had been thoroughly made over. It had, but damage control was clearly the name of the game. Bewildered Lincoln executives could only shake their heads and unwrap the hatchet.

This lack of clear vision goes deeper than a tactical mistake with one car. All was not well at Ford Motor Company. Since the departure of Robert McNamara to the Kennedy administration, where he would attempt to do to the Vietcong what he had done to the Thunderbird, Lee Iacocca was the golden boy in Dearborn.

As company president in the 1970s, the blunt, charismatic, often profane Iacocca had scored major triumphs in the car business, and had done more than a little mischief. After Bunkie Knudsen was brought in to run the company in 1968, Iacocca instituted a guerrilla warfare campaign against him, and soon Bunkie was out the door. When a fretful Henry Ford II began to dislike Iacocca in the mid-1970s and introduced Philip Caldwell to the top executive level of the company, Ia-

This 1970 Continental two-door shows off the all-new body-work for 1970. The bladelike quality of the fenders is empha-sized again, and the rear of the roof follows a new fastback line to the high rear deck. *Credit: Ford Motor Company*

cocca escalated to open hostilities. Often Caldwell and Iacocca toured the design studios at different times of day, each of them rejecting what the other had approved, leaving confused and frustrated stylists and engineers in their wake.

During the late 1970s, this chaos at Ford was echoed in the lack of firm and confident direction in Lincoln too. The glory days of the '61 Continental and the Mark III were past, long past by Detroit time. While sales were still respectable, the quality of the products and their distinctive Ford character had slipped, leaving buyers unsatisfied and car lines generally ailing. Add to this the growing amount of government regulation, near panic over oil shortages, the threat of gasoline rationing, the growing presence of Asian imports, and you have a picture of a company suffering from extreme anxiety.

Something had to give, and it did. In July 1978, Henry Ford II announced the separation of Lee Iacocca

from Ford Motor Company and, sometime later, the elevation of Philip Caldwell to the position of chairman, the first non-Ford family member ever to hold the position. Once again, Henry II had saved the company from disaster. And once again, the company was completely reorganized, from top executive positions down to the middle managers of the divisions. For Lincoln, the future looked bright, but meaningful change would take time.

It came to pass that 1979 was the last year for the full-sized Fords and Lincolns. To commemorate the occasion, a special collectible Continental was offered; it was the last of its kind. A new smaller car would debut with the new decade in 1980. This special edition was perhaps cynically called the Collector's Series, and offered an especially lush package of features. As word spread that smaller Lincolns were coming, sales accelerated until, by the end of the model year, they had reached an astonishing 113,607 total.

The continuing success of the Designer and Collector's Series Lincolns spawned this well-equipped 1979 Town Car Collector's Series. In the last year of the full-sized car, the Collector's Series Town Car was truly the last of a vanishing breed. This vehicle came in Midnight Blue metallic or Frost White, with an illuminated entry system, tilt steering wheel, automatic garage door opener, cruise control, and a gold anodized grille. It cost $12,093, and 76,458 were sold. *Credit: Ford Motor Company*

This is the original 1977-1/2 Versailles. In 1978, sales of the Versailles plummeted to 8,931, about half of its first year's figure. The plunging sales figures triggered some kind of ah-ooo-gah alarm in Ford headquarters, and for '79, the Versailles looked like it had been thoroughly made over. It had, but damage control was clearly the name of the game. *Credit: Ford Motor Company*

Chapter 5

Lincoln Today—The 1980s and 1990s

Looking back, it's easy to underestimate the turmoil of the American car business in the 1980s. Detroit did the right thing by downsizing its products, but those first smaller cars were little short of awful. The combination of a recession at the beginning of the Reagan era and customers genuinely rejecting what Detroit had to offer left the domestic car business in shambles. Looking back, we see this as a transitional time; then it looked like Armageddon.

Lincoln was not immune to this malaise. For 1980, the pride of Ford Motor Company sold only 74,908 vehicles, less than two-thirds of its level from the year be-

The Continental line has been an integral and influential part of Lincoln's heritage for more than 50 years.

1940 — Edsel Ford's one-off Continental was so popular it led to the 1940 production car.

1946 — The postwar Continental coupes sported trademark rear-mounted spares and smooth, uncluttered design.

1956 — The expensive, exclusive Continental Mark II had a production run of under 3000 in 1956 and 1957.

1958 — Despite its size, the 1958 – 1960 Continental's big V-8 and new suspension made it a good performer.

1964 — The clean-lined Continental that debuted in 1961 is regarded as a trendsetter in American auto design.

1971 — Continental's well-established styling hallmarks were carried over into the 1970s.

1982 — The Continental of 1982 through 1985 featured an electronic air suspension that presaged the sophistication of today's Continentals.

1988 — The V-6 powered 1988 Continental's sales quickly exceeded production capacity for Lincoln's highest sales year ever.

1995 — The 1995 Continental brings together trend-setting engineering with customer-oriented features that echo back to the original Continental.

The popular Town Car option for the Continental burst from its chains in 1981 and became a separate Lincoln model of its own, replacing the Continental in the line-up. The option package that had been the Town Car was now called the Signature Series. *Credit: Ford Motor Company*

Next page, photographed at the exclusive LaQuinta Hotel in Palm Springs, California, this 1984 Continental must be used to living the good life. By the mid-1980s, the United States was booming in the center of the Reagan era, and Lincoln owners demanded and got the best car for their dollars. *Credit: Ford Motor Company*

Entering a new formal phase, this 1982 Continental represents a short-term experiment with neoclassic styling that affected the whole domestic industry in the early 1980s. Cadillac, Lincoln, and Chrysler all tried some version of this theme, based on the "bustleback" Hooper coachwork of some 1930s Rolls-Royce automobiles. *Credit: Ford Motor Company*

fore. Fortunately, the cars themselves were better than their sales numbers indicate. Some of this vertical drop in sales can be attributed to a management gaffe: the end of the Marks as a recognizably separate car line from mainstream Lincolns.

For 1980, the Mark VI was little more than another Lincoln two- or four-door, albeit with some special body panels and trim items. The exclusive look and feel of the Mark was gone. It was a lesson that Lincoln would learn in red ink, the most effective teacher in the car business.

The 1980 designs represented a general backsliding from the simple classicism of the 1960s and the brash dynamics of the '70s. For example, the Lincoln Conti-

nental coupe used a full B-pillar design, which, with the exception of the big Continental coupe of 1975-1979, hadn't been seen on a Lincoln since the early '50s. Side window glass in the Continental was fully framed, another step backwards in appearance. Furthermore, it was hard for buyers to accept that a $9,000 Mercury looked so much like a $15,000 Lincoln. While the mid-size Versailles was changed and dressed-up more for 1980 than any other year, this was its last hurrah. The struggling bantamweight sold a mere 4,784 vehicles. In part, this was due to an inflated price of $15,664 for the plain-Jane four-door. The Versailles' successor would have a much better time of it in the brave new world of the 1980s.

Nearing the end of its product cycle, this 1986 Continental still looks good in motion. For 1986, the Continental, with a 5.0 ltr V-8, received the addition of multi-port fuel injection and a corresponding boost from 140 to 150hp. Continental also added the premium Ford JBL sound system for this year.

Having abandoned the 460 and 400ci engines in 1978 and 1979, the new Lincolns were powered by the corporate 302ci (5.0ltr) V-8 with 351 Windsor (5.7ltr) engines as an optional upgrade for the Continentals and Marks. In Lincoln applications, the 302 used electronic fuel injection, and the 351 had a compromised EEC III system, known as central fuel injection (CFI). Don't be fooled by the name; this was simply the Ford equivalent of GM's Computer Controlled Carburetor. It was based on a carburetor body under rudimentary electronic management. Eventually Ford and Lincoln became world leaders in electronic fuel injection, but at that time it was one step forward, two steps back. A new automatic, the well-engineered AOD four-speed with overdrive, became standard equipment in 1980 and continued to be a part of the Lincoln mechanical package for years to come.

The popular Town Car option for the Continental burst from its chains for 1981 and became a separate Lincoln model of its own, replacing the Continental in the line-up. The option package that had been the Town Car was now called the Signature Series. The six-tieth anniversary of Lincoln was an auspicious occasion in 1981, along with mildly recovered sales. The only sour note was the continued decline of sales for the Mark. Now that this line had lost its athletic design and exclusivity, it was clearly not as appealing as before. Prices for the model year reflected the inflation that was causing a continued recession in the economy overall. Town Cars cost $13,707 for the two-door and $14,068 for the four-door. Continental Mark VIs cost $16,858 for the coupe and $17,303 for the sedan, with the Signature variants going for $22,463 and $22,838. The weight of these cars was nearly identical to the 1980 models but about 800lb below the mass of the full-sized Lincolns of the 1970s.

Stop me if you've heard this one before. Lincoln had a mission to become a leader in airbag technology, one of the best safety innovations of the modern era. To gather airbag field data without putting the buying public at risk, a fleet of twenty-five Lincoln Continental Mark VIs painted Light Fawn metallic were loaned to the Dearborn Police Department for about fifteen months. The cars included large police shield decals on

After coasting along as the least improved and most tradition bound of Lincoln's offerings, the venerable Town Car was reskinned and much improved for 1985. Even bigger changes were on the drawing board for the future. *Credit: Ford Motor Company*

the doors and lettering that said "Police" on the front fenders. Blue flashing lights were artfully concealed inside the body of the cars. Citizens were alternately amused and outraged, thinking the police department

of Dearborn, Michigan, had actually bought Lincolns for its own use. What an echo of the Roaring '20s! In all the time these cars were on the road, only one of them was involved in a collision substantial enough to cause the air bag to deploy. It makes you wonder if the cops in these elegant police cars had gold-plated handcuffs. I'm sure they had some interesting stories to tell.

Making quite a splash for 1982 was an all-new Continental. Trim and stylish, the new Continental was clearly the successor to the unlamented Versailles; but, unlike the Versailles, which offered warmed-over Mercury styling, this new Continental was a radical departure from the Ford norm. It was also obviously based on a theme from GM, as Lincoln again exercised its wannabe status.

In 1980, Cadillac gave its original generation Seville a radical new body shell including a truncated rear end (no pun intended). To car buffs, the treatment was obvious—it was a repetition of the Hooper "bustle-back" coachbuilt bodies seen on Rolls-Royce and Bentleys from the late 1920s through the 1930s. It was, in fact, the kind of "continental" design element Edsel so admired.

Nevertheless, Cadillac buyers did not care for this styling device. The 1980 Seville did not sell in numbers like the 1982 Continental sold. Throughout the 1980s, Cadillac suffered one embarrassment after another, notably, their diesel engine program, their V-8-6-4 engines, and worst of all, the compact Cimarron. Part of Lincoln's unrestrained success in the 1980s was due to Cadillac buyers jumping ship and buying Lincoln, because Cadillac had let them down.

The new Continental used design cues from that Classic era in the razor-edge treatment of the C-pillar and the lines of the trunk and also in the graceful, curving character line that swept back from the front end to the tall taillights. It was not a perfect design, but a striking one, all the same.

Based on the Mustang's "Fox" platform, the new design took advantage of advanced engineering facilities and various computer aids in shaping the body and floor pan structures. The 1982 Continental was a five-passenger, front-engine, rear-drive vehicle. It was 201.2in long on a 108.6in wheelbase. It was 73.6in wide and 54.9in tall. Weight was modest for a Lincoln, 3512lb, about 150lb less than the Versailles it replaced. It was powered by Ford's corporate 5.0ltr V-8, the same engine used in the Mustang, in, of course, a different state of tune. The 3.8ltr V-6 was available as an option, but few V-6 Continentals sold. Nitrogen gas shock absorbers, popular in Europe and effective in combining good ride and handling, were used on this new Continental. The AOD automatic was standard equipment, as were four-wheel disc brakes.

Inside were reclining, power front seats and an electronic instrument panel with message center, a feature that Lincoln executed much better than Cadillac in the same time period. Other luxury features included automatic temperature control and an all-electronic AM/FM stereo radio.

For 1983, the new Continental, the popular Town Car, and the Mark VI soldiered on with no real changes, although the Signature and Designer Series options were shuffled around, giving more equipment to the base cars, and trading some colors and other trim touches. As the Reagan years continued, demand for large, luxury cars grew, and Lincoln was the choice of more buyers than ever before, as Cadillac lost direction and product quality.

In the mid-1980s, the Mark VII brought aerodynamic styling to Lincoln and a return to performance that had been missing for years as Ford engineers struggled with smog regulations and federal CAFE standards for fuel economy.

The 1984 Continental picked up some technical innovations from the Mark VIII, with which it shared the versatile Fox platform. These changes included an auto-leveling air suspension, quicker steering, an improved electronic instrument panel, and the all-American return of the horn button to the center of the steering wheel pad from (a perversely European touch) the turn signal stalk.

After coasting along as the least-improved and most tradition bound of Lincoln's offerings, the venerable Town Car was mildly reskinned and improved noticeably for 1985. The once razor-edge Town Car had its corners rounded off and was sleeker and more handsome than before. Even bigger changes were on the drawing board for the future. The new Town Car continued many of the previous version's styling cues. Indeed, below the beltline it looked almost the same, but a new greenhouse improved interior room and revamped the proportions of the Town Car. With more unsuccessful models coming from Cadillac, the Town Car captured an ever larger market share, and sales continued to climb, reaching 119,878.

Despite relatively quiet years in 1986 and 1987, Lincoln designers were burning the midnight oil and

Next page, while the Town Car for 1986 was little changed on the outside, it offered sequential multi-port fuel injection for the 5.0ltr V-8 engine and a Ford JBL premium audio system featuring twelve high quality JBL speakers. The redesigned Town Car set sales records in 1985 and virtually matched those numbers in 1986. *Credit: Ford Motor Company*

Based on the popular Taurus platform, the 1988 Continental was criticized for using a 3.8ltr V-6, but the car was quiet, comfortable, and relaxing to drive. This Continental was very popular with buyers and set a new standard for rental cars. *Credit: Ford Motor Company*

had products in the wings that could be the best Lincolns of all time. These vehicles would be cars that were worthy of a worldwide reputation, cars that Henry Leland and Edsel Ford would have appreciated.

A surprisingly competent new Continental, based on the popular Taurus/Sable platform, went on the market for 1988. Sleek and modern, this car was still identifiable as a Lincoln and in no way betrayed its middle-class origins. It was Lincoln's first ever front-wheel drive vehicle, a true history maker for the division. The new

The 1990 Town Car features exciting, modern design both inside and out, an assortment of major functional improvements, and traditional full-size luxury, roominess, and ride. This Signature Series continues as a feature-packed edition of the car. *Credit: Ford Motor Company*

Another version of the 1990 Town Car is this Cartier Designer Series. Even in this considerable redesign, the Town Car still offers six-passenger comfort and the largest trunk in its class. Sales of this new vehicle jumped 14 percent over the previous year. *Credit: Ford Motor Company*

Continental was larger than the Taurus and heavier, representing a slight stretch of that platform.

Where the Taurus had a 106in wheelbase and 190in overall length, the Continental boasted a 109in wheelbase and measured 206in bumper to bumper. The new Continental, with its 3.8ltr V-6, weighed 4093lb, compared to the Taurus/Sable weight of 3135lb with the 3.0ltr V-6. In its second year of pro-

duction, the new Continental featured standard dual air bags, one for the driver and one for the passenger, baby, or dog—whoever was riding in the right-hand seat. This leading-edge safety feature set off a rush among other American cars to include dual air bags as part of their resume.

For model year 1990, a new Town Car rolled out to a very positive reception. Smoother and more rounded than the 1988 restyle, this new vehicle retained rear-wheel drive and included many easily identifiable Lincoln styling clues while giving the decade-old Town Car a look that could easily continue through the 1990s. The new Town Car is a remarkably handsome vehicle. It continues the large greenhouse look of the 1985 Town Car, yet it softens all of the familiar body lines into one smooth shape.

So outstanding and engaging was this new Town Car that it became the first luxury sedan in thirty-eight years to capture the prestigious *Motor Trend* Car of the Year award. Here, the famous golden caliper is presented to Ross Roberts, (right) Ford vice president and Lincoln-Mercury general manager, by Bob Brown, senior VP of Petersen Publishing Company, the parent company of *Motor Trend* magazine. *Credit: Ford Motor Company*

This author recalls the press conference that launched the new Town Car, where Lincoln designers said with obvious relief that they had labored mightily to create a car that would appeal to traditional Lincoln buyers, who were typically in their fifties or sixties, and yet make the car more fuel efficient and quieter than ever before.

They certainly achieved that last goal. The Lincoln Town Car is now the quietest running car on the American road and among the quietest in the world. It is a noble return to the roots of these fine cars.

In 1991, the Town Car acquired Ford's superb new modular V-8, measuring 4.6ltr. This sohc engine is part of a family of motors, all using the same bore spacing. They can be interchangeably machined on the same assembly line, drastically reducing tooling costs and making it much easier to produce a new motor to match a car platform or to make changes of displacement and configuration in an existing engine.

It was now the Mark's turn to be freshened. For 1993, the new Mark VIII greeted an amazed public and press. While it shocked some, it pleased the true car lover in many. Sleek and highly aerodynamic, this update of the Mark was as technically advanced as it was aerodynamic.

The next Lincoln product to be prepared for life in the twenty-first century was the Continental. Announced as a 1995 model, the new Continental is a stunning showcase of advanced design and technology. One of the most technically advanced cars ever produced by a domestic manufacturer, the new Continental truly carries on in the spirit of the first Edsel Ford Continental. But where the original Continental wowed its fans with world-class styling, the new 1995 version offers a dazzling array of high-tech features and exerts a different kind of hypnotic attraction.

So much is new about this car that it's fair to say it is a completely remade vehicle. It uses a different unibody design than the previous generation Continental and is powered by a variant of the 4.6ltr V-8 that performs so brilliantly in the Mark VIII. However, this new engine, known as the InTech™ V-8 (for Intelligent Technology) is transversely mounted and drives the front wheels. This front-wheel-drive, front transverse engine layout is nearly the only common element between the previous Continental and the new generation.

Continued on page 117

1995 CONTINENTAL SPECIFICATIONS

Engine
Type: 4.6ltr, 32-valve, four-cam, all-aluminum V-8
Fuel-injection: Electronic
Engine control system: EEC-V module
Induction system: SEFI
Battery: 12-volt, 84amp
Alternator: 130amp
Cooling system: Standard recovery 50/50
Cylinder head material: Aluminum
Block material: Cast-Aluminum
Valve operation: Hydraulic
Camshaft drive: Chain
Displacement: 281ci/4.6ltr
Bore: 90.2mm/3.60in
Stroke: 90mm/3.60in *sic*
Compression ratio: 9.85:1
Horsepower (SAE net): 260 @ 5750rpm
Torque: 265lb-ft @ 4750rpm
Recommended fuel: Premium unleaded

Transmission
Type: AX4N four-speed electronic automatic
Gear ratios:
>1st: 2.77
>2nd: 1.54
>3rd: 1.00
>4th: 0.69
>Reverse: 2.26

Final drive: 3.56:1
Special features: Overdrive fourth gear, non synchronous shift, lock-up
torque converter, electronic control from EEC-V

Dimensions/Capacities
Exterior
Length: 206.3in
Wheelbase: 109.0in
Curb weight: 3969lb
Width: 73.3in
Track, front: 63.0in
Track, rear: 61.5in
Height: 55.9in
Ground clearance: 8.9in (at front bumper)

Interior
EPA volume index: 102.7cu-ft
Seating capacity: 5 to 6 adults
Front
Leg room: 41.8in
Hip room: 55.5in
Head room: 39.1in
Shoulder room: 57.2in
Rear
Leg room: 39.2in
Hip room: 56.5in
Knee room: 5.0in
Head room: 38.0in
Shoulder room: 56.6in
Luggage compartment capacity: 18.1cu-ft
Liftover height: 27.2in
Fuel tank: 18.0 gallons

Chassis/Body
Structure: Unitized, all-steel welded body–separate front subframe
Bumper system: 5mph, polypropylene facings on bonded front,
polycarbonate bonded rear
Anticorrosion: Two-sided galvanized steel, E-coat, phosphate spray
Safety features: Front and rear crush zones, reinforced structure, dual air
bags, ABS, available traction control
Coefficient of drag: 0.32

Suspension
Front: Independent MacPherson Strut with forged aluminum lower arms,
strut-mounted air springs, and 19mm antiroll bar, Firestone air springs,

Sachs gas-pressurized/hydraulic struts
Rear: Independent, short and long control arm, Firestone air springs, Sachs gas-pressurized/hydraulic shock absorbers (Quad-shocks), 19.5mm antiroll bar

Steering
Type: Integral rack and pinion
Assist: Variable effort hydraulic
Overall ratio: 16:95 center–12:2 at stops
Steering wheel diameter: 15in
Turns lock-to-lock: 2.86
Turning circle: 41.1ft

Brakes
Assist: Four-wheel hydraulic
Front: 249mm ventilated disc
Rear: 256mm solid disc
ABS: ITT Teves four-channel integral hydraulic/electric
Swept area: 261.5sq-in front, 141.6sq-in rear

Tires/Wheels
Tire size: P255/60R-16
Inflation: 32psi front, 30psi rear
Spare: T125/80R-16 compact spare
Wheel diameter: 16in
Wheel width: 7in

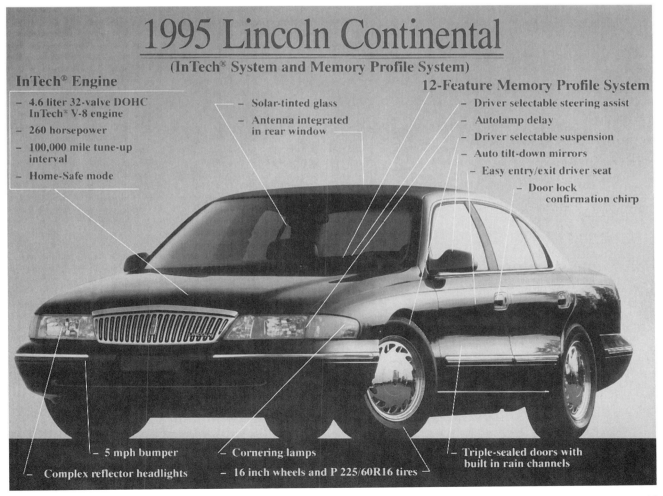

1995 Lincoln Continental
(InTech® System and Memory Profile System)

InTech® Engine
- 4.6 liter 32-valve DOHC InTech® V-8 engine
- 260 horsepower
- 100,000 mile tune-up interval
- Home-Safe mode

- Solar-tinted glass
- Antenna integrated in rear window

12-Feature Memory Profile System
- Driver selectable steering assist
- Autolamp delay
- Driver selectable suspension
- Auto tilt-down mirrors
- Easy entry/exit driver seat
- Door lock confirmation chirp

- 5 mph bumper
- Complex reflector headlights
- Cornering lamps
- 16 inch wheels and P 225/60R16 tires
- Triple-sealed doors with built in rain channels

As the very newest Lincoln, this 1995 Continental represents some of the most advanced engineering available in an American luxury car. What this X-ray drawing doesn't reveal is the high degree of electronic sophistication in the vehicle or its ability to be programmed to match the tastes of radically different drivers. *Credit: Ford Motor Company*

Moving the Continental slightly upscale and adding InTech™ V-8 power makes this 1995 version a sophisticated and enjoyable car. Design elements resemble the recent Mark VIII with its dramatic grille and sculptured sides, but advanced electronics and programmability give this car a personality of its own. *Credit: Ford Motor Company*

timate interior space and leisurely performance, emphasizing luxury and comfort. His Continental–the same car–is roomier, more aggressive on the road, and handles more like a touring car than a cruiser. The same scenario might also pertain to older and younger buyers, all of whom have different tastes and expectations in their vehicle. Like no other car on the road today, the Continental can meet those diverse expectations.

This vehicle offers perhaps more programmability than any other luxury product in history. Program the fit of the interior, the ride quality, even the level of performance, and then you are ready to drive. If anything makes the 1995 Continental stand out, it is its ability to conform to the needs and desires of its owner. In the future, many more cars will be made this way; for now, it is only a small codicil in the legacy of Lincoln.

Beneath that long, elegantly curved hood, the 1995 Continental breaks new ground for Ford Motor Company. It is the first Ford product ever to place a V-8 in

Fully instrumented, the 1995 Continental offers the driver unprecedented control of the vehicle. Ride, transmission, handling, and interior setup can all be programmed to match the needs of two different drivers. *Credit: Ford Motor Company*

Continued from page 113

The most remarkable aspect of the new Continental is its ability to be an automotive chameleon. Audio, steering, seating, and several other functions can be programmed to suit an individual driver–two, in fact. A dominant theme of the car is its ability to be "reprogrammed" to suit different tastes, even different owners. Drivers of the car, although they have a large menu of choices to consider, can customize ride, handling, comfort, and responsiveness to a degree never before possible.

It's conceivable that a man and woman who buy a new Continental together could effectively have two cars for the price of one. Hers is soft riding, with an in-

With excellent fit and finish, the 1995 Continental is the engineering equivalent of any of the fine European import cars. As this pose suggests, the car is appearing at country clubs across the nation. *Credit: Ford Motor Company*

the transverse mounting position. Possibly a response to Cadillac's Northstar System, the InTech™ system features a variation on the superb modular 4.6ltr engine that first saw service in the Lincoln Town Car, in sohc form, and then provided the abundant power, in dohc form, for the sleek Mark VIII.

The new Continental uses the all-aluminum dohc version of this engine, with extra soundproofing added to the motor itself, including Teflon-coated pistons, an oil pan made from a metal-plastic-metal sandwich material, and a high-flow conical air filter. This engine makes 260hp and 265lb-ft of torque at peak.

This healthy and efficient motor is coupled to an advanced four-speed overdrive automatic transmission, the AX4N transaxle. Both engine and tranny are controlled by the EEC-V computer, now with 112K of onboard memory—twice that of the previous generation EEC-IV. Distinguishing this new gearbox is a non synchronous shifting feature that allows quicker downshifts from third gear to second and third gear to first, and smoother upshifts from second gear to third. The AX4N is built in Ford's Van Dyke transmission plant in Sterling Heights, Michigan.

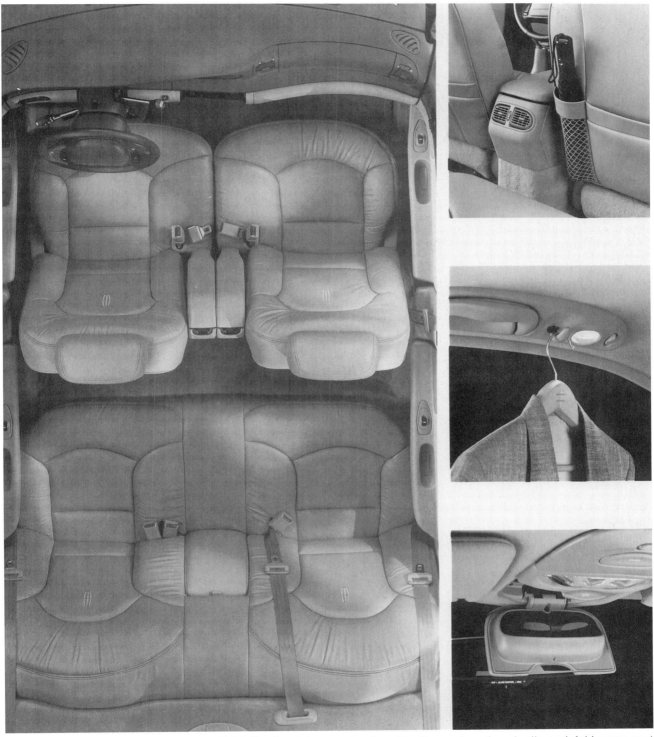

Seen from above, the interior of the 1995 Continental holds five or six passengers and has some wonderful touches like the on-board umbrella and fold-away coat hooks. *Credit: Ford Motor Company*

Chapter 6

Lincoln Engines—The V-12s and V-8, the Modular V-8 In the New Town Car, and the Mark VIII

From the beginning, Lincoln cars had superb engines, even if their chassis and bodies were not always as accomplished. It was, after all, the Lelands' experience and success in building automobile engines for Ransom E. Olds

that lured them into the car business in the first place.

It was in engine building that old Henry Leland's passion for precision had the greatest impact. An engine built to more precise tolerances will always be a better

The Mark VII is not only a fast car, but a good handler as well. Part of that good road holding is due to the electronic air springs used exclusively by the Mark VII.

Manufactured by Goodyear, the air suspension system became a Lincoln engineering trademark. *Credit: Goodyear News Bureau Photo*

This air strut was planned as a development of the Mark VII's air suspension but never came to pass in exactly this form. That is the Ford Probe IV in the background. *Credit: Goodyear News Bureau Photo*

performing engine. In the case of running gear and bodywork, this is not necessarily so.

The Lelands had a major impact on automotive engine building even before the First World War, as demonstrated when Cadillac won the Dewar Trophy in 1908 for the interchangeability of parts. Three Cadillacs were taken completely apart at the Brooklands race track in England, their parts mixed and jumbled, then reassembled. All three cars ran perfectly. It was a feat previously impossible in the largely hand-fitted world of auto manufacture in those days.

Lincoln cars began life in the shadow of the World War I Liberty airplane engine, which had been built by the Lelands, father & son, in a burst of patriotic fervor. A move that cost them so dearly in the years after the war. The Liberty engine was a purebred V-12, and so the first Lincolns were also proudly V-12 powered. Edsel Ford maintained the V-12 tradition during his years as the head of Lincoln, but the economic pressures of the postwar era and the availability of some of the best

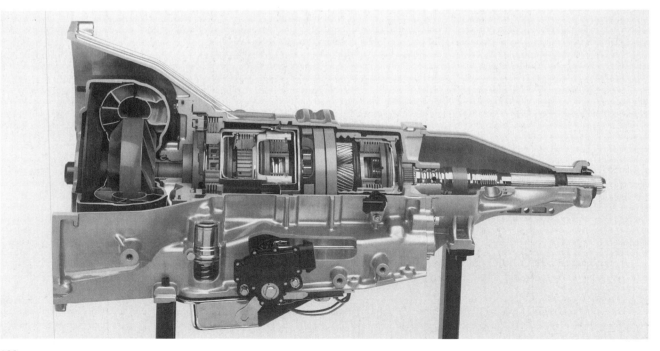

TRANSMISSION OPERATING TEMPERATURE (TOT)

OTHER VEHICLE SUB SYSTEMS

POWERTRAIN ELECTRONIC CONTROL MODULE (EEC IV)

BULKHEAD WIRING CONNECTOR

TOT
EPC
MCCC
SS1/SS2

OUTPUT SHAFT SPEED SENSOR (OSS)
MODULATED CONVERTER CLUTCH CONTROL (MCCC)
SHIFT SOLENOID #1 (SS1)
SHIFT SOLENOID #2 (SS2)
ELECTRONIC PRESSURE CONTROL SOLENOID (EPC)
MANUAL LEVER POSITION SENSOR (MLPS)

INPUTS	POWERTRAIN ELECTRONIC CONTROL MODULE (EEC IV)	OUTPUTS
OUTPUT SHAFT SPEED SENSOR (OSS)*		ELECTRONIC PRESSURE CONTROL SOLENOID (EPC)*
MASS AIR FLOW (MAF)		MODULATED CONVERTER CLUTCH CONTROL (MCCC)*
AIR CHARGE TEMPERATURE (ACT)		SHIFT SOLENOID #1 (SS1)*
THROTTLE POSITION (TP)		SHIFT SOLENOID #2 (SS2)*
AIR CONDITIONING CLUTCH (ACC)		
ENGINE COOLANT TEMPERATURE (ECT)		
BRAKE ON/OFF SWITCH (BOO)		
PROFILE IGNITION PICKUP (PIP) SIGNAL FROM EDIS MODULE		
TRANSMISSION OPERATING TEMPERATURE (TOT)*		
MANUAL LEVER POSITION SENSOR (MLP)*		
TRANSMISSION CONTROL SWITCH (TCS)		

*TRANSMISSION SENSORS AND ACTUATORS

MAY 1, 1992

This page, designed especially for the Mark VIII, this AODE transmission features an unusually high level of communication with the engine master computer, the EEC IV module. *Credit: Ford Motor Company*

The first of a new family of engines from Ford, this sohc 4.6ltr V-8 is one of the "modular" engines that feature a common bore spacing and can all be machined on the same assembly line whether they are four, six, or eight cylinders. First used in the Town Car in 1990, this new engine offers a high-tech approach to the traditional V-8. *Credit: Ford Motor Company*

American V-8 technology from Ford Motor Company, along with the collapse of demand for V-12-powered automobiles, eventually led to the adoption of V-8 power for Lincolns.

While some may look upon this as a disaster or a come-down, it bears remembering that the Lincolns that were so dominant in the Carrera Panamericana road race in the early 1950s were V-8 powered and of only moderate displacement. And, the best performing Lincoln of all time, the new Mark VIII, is powered by a 280hp 4.6ltr V-8 (to be examined in detail later in this chapter) that is among the most sophisticated pas-

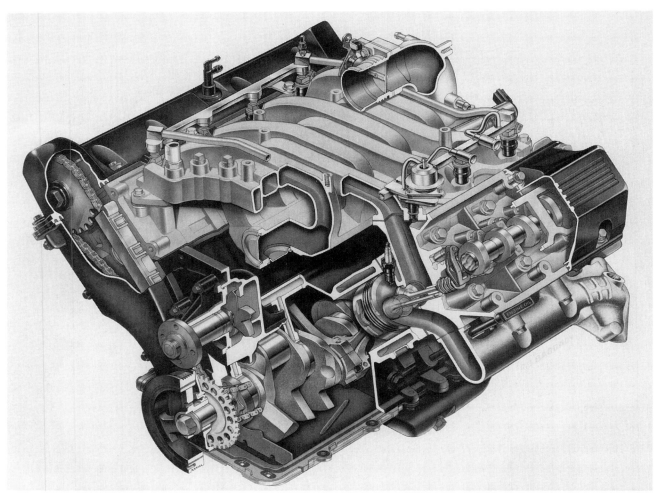

Inside, this engine shows that it is a mix of old technology (two valves per cylinder, 90deg layout, log-type exhaust manifold) with the new throttle body fuel injection, cross-ram manifold, and so on. *Credit: Ford Motor Company*

senger car engines on the road today and a fitting successor to the tradition of the Lelands themselves. It is also the best mass produced engine to come from Ford's advanced engineering department.

Let's begin our study of Lincoln power with a look at those V-12s from the Zephyr era—the early 1940s—and work our way up to the modular V-8 in the Mark VIII of the early 1990s.

Although the Zephyr represented an advanced body design for its time, it did not have an engine of equal sophistication. The Zephyr nearly got a V-8 until Edsel had an attack of conscience one day and instructed chief engineer Frank Johnson to draft a new V-12 engine, essentially by adding four cylinders onto the existing Ford V-8. Unfortunately, this motor was never a winner. It was a side-valve engine based on a 75deg V but with only four main bearings. From a 3.75x2.75in bore and stroke, the engine displaced 267ci. It pro-

duced 110 to 120hp at an athletic 3800rpm—adequate, but not an overwhelming figure for the period. However, the engine's strong 180lb-ft of torque gave the Zephyr good acceleration and helped to make up for the motor's rough idle and tendency to overheat. For 1942, this engine was bored out by 1/16in per cylinder, resulting in a displacement of 305ci. In this configuration, it produced roughly 130hp.

Also in '42, the Zephyr was offered with Lincoln's optional $189 semi-automatic transmission, Liquamatic. Heavy and quite complex, this disaster was built by, and perhaps designed by, Warner Gear. Liquamatic included a three-speed gearbox, shifted by vacuum servos, an overdrive rear axle, and a fluid-filled drive coupling. Not only did this unit fail to work in the field, but it was so difficult to service that Lincoln was forced to recall all vehicles so equipped and refit them with manual transmissions. For a company that prided itself on

Take that 4.6ltr block, cast it in aluminum, add four-valve aluminum heads and quad cams, and you have the dohc version of the 4.6ltr V-8. First used in the Mark VIII, this engine, in a slightly different form, also appears in the 1995 Continental. Featuring hollow camshafts, silent chain cam drives, an inverted plenum, and accessory mounting points cast directly into the block, this beauty is the most high-tech engine a Lincoln has had since the Leland V-12. *Credit: Ford Motor Company*

technical leadership, this was a bitter pill to swallow. Edsel was not pleased. The added stress of this embarrassment made his stomach pains all but unbearable.

Quickly, Liquamatic was soon forgotten with the news of Pearl Harbor and America's entry into World War II. Production of all Lincolns ceased in February 1942 while the entire Ford organization shifted over to making war products.

When Lincoln production resumed in 1946, the 305ci V-12 was again pressed into service but, by this time, Lincoln engineers discovered that they had overbored the engine, and the thinner cylinder walls were not reliable. Consequently, they returned to the 267ci configuration, but increased compression so that the engine produced 125bhp and 214lb-ft of torque. This engine continued through the 1947 model year. As these motors aged, they showed considerable oil consumption and blow-by. Many an owner was plagued by the sight of an oil-filmed and filthy engine compartment, even in a freshly tuned car. Many mechanics resorted to bizarre combinations of vacuum pipes and hoses to alleviate the oil misting problems, but most of these fixes simply routed oil mist into the cylinders, causing a sooty exhaust.

With market demand so strong, Lincoln management decided the time was right for a shift to V-8 power in 1948. But, they made the cost-conscious decision of choosing their Lincoln engine from the ranks of Ford

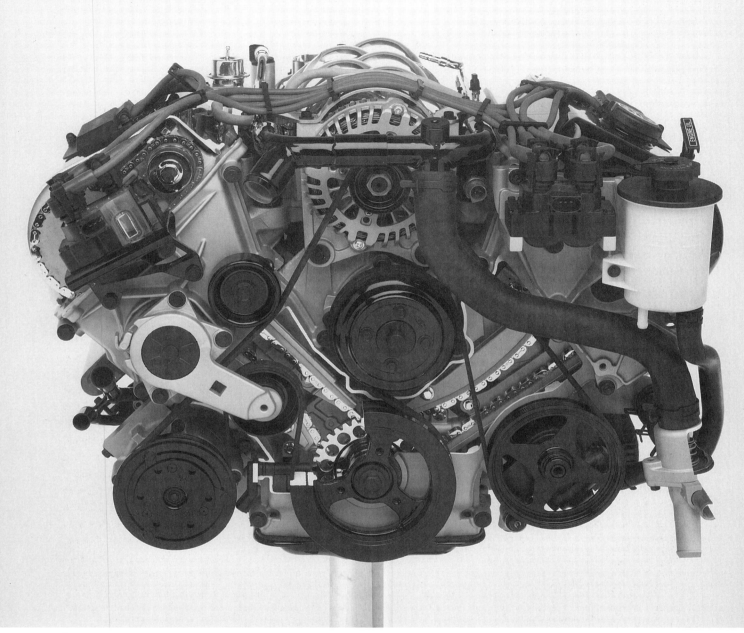

Compactness is one of the major virtues of this engine. Notice how tightly packaged it is, to enable low hood lines and maximum room for front wheel articulation. Notice the complex path of the front serpentine accessory drive belt. If this one belt goes, you lose power steering, alternator, oil and water pumps, and—worst of all—air conditioning! *Credit: Ford Motor Company*

truck motors. An era had truly ended.

This new "EQ" or "Rouge" V-8 was designed by C.C. Johnson and resembled other Ford heavy-duty blocks of the time. It had a bore and stroke of 3.5x4.375in for an overall displacement of 336.7ci. With compression set at 7.1:1, the low-revving motor produced 152hp at 3600rpm, but a hefty 225lb-ft of torque. A stump puller indeed! Powered by this engine, Lincolns were among the fastest American cars of their era. A Cosmopolitan could actually break the ton (100mph), with a top speed of 102mph. The EQ engine suffered some problems at first, including camshaft wear and cracks in the cylinder heads, both metallurgical problems traced to the Ford foundry and eventually corrected. The large intake valves in this motor caused a rough idle, so new, softer motor mounts were installed after the first few months of production to compensate.

Lincoln's new chief engineer, Earle S. MacPherson, after whom the MacPherson strut front suspension is named (since he invented it), was not thrilled with the EQ engine and wasted no time in developing an excellent new powerplant for the 1952 model year. This new engine was the first Lincoln overhead valve motor and the first of Ford's famous "Y-block" engine family. The Lincolns that won the Carrera Panamericana used this same motor, in slightly modified form, running it at 5000rpm for long distances.

The new engine was neither an exotic nor an unusual powerplant, simply a very good one. It was an all-iron, 90deg V-8, featuring a 3.8x3.5in bore and stroke. Overall displacement was 317.5ci and compression was 7.5:1. It used an in-head combustion chamber with substantial squish area, so the action took place in the space below the valve heads. This was fine for producing even, fast burns and low knock.

With a two-barrel downdraft carburetor, this engine produced 160hp at 3900rpm. But the potential existed for much more power from this motor, as time would prove. Lincoln engineers gave special attention to breathing in their first ohv engine and were pleased by its performance. They also tried to make it easy to service, placing the oil pump on the outside of the block and the fuel pump near the front of the engine where air flow from the fan would keep it running cool.

In 1953, the engine received a four-barrel carburetor, bigger intake valves, longer intake runners on the manifold, and a boost in compression to 8.0:1. The result was 205bhp at 4200rpm, with an associated increase of torque to 305lb-ft at 2800rpm— more than a 25 percent bump in horsepower. The four-barrel carburetor used a progressive vacuum linkage (the secondary barrels activated only when the primaries were nearly wide open and manifold vacuum exceeded a preset level), so driveability was retained while performance was greatly enhanced. This raised top speed to 115mph. It was this package that raced in the Carrera Panamericana.

For most of the 1950s this outstanding V-8 continued in service, increasing displacement and horsepower as the years progressed. In 1955, the engine was bored out by .014 to 3.94in, which brought displacement up to 341ci. With compression raised to 8.5:1, it now delivered 225bhp and 332lb-ft of torque. Dual exhausts also

helped in producing the higher horsepower figure by slightly lowering back pressure in the exhaust manifold.

The increased engine power for 1955 was desirable, certainly, but it was also necessary to offset frictional losses caused by the new Turbo-Drive automatic transmission. In previous years, Lincoln had installed Hydra-Matic transmissions from GM, with the idea that it would offer its own automatic when the time was right and funds were available.

Using a fluid torque converter and planetary gear set, the Turbo-Drive started out in second gear (like most automatics of the day) and would only engage first when it kicked-down under hard acceleration. While it was better than the ineffectual Liquamatic of the prewar years, Turbo-Drive was not nearly as smooth or driver-friendly as the GM gearbox. One advantage was that it offered a better shift quadrant than Hydra-Matic, with reverse following park, not drive. This engine and transmission combination was used on all Lincoln models of the period.

Larger Lincolns demanded bigger engines. The 1952 V-8 received a near complete overhaul for 1956. While it may have been a thorough makeover, this was still the solid, high-revving 90deg V-8 that had served Lincoln so well through the early 1950s. Modifications included changes to the block, crank, cam, and oil pump. The engine was bored out again and now displaced 368ci with 9.0:1 compression. Combined with a larger four-barrel carburetor, the engine now had an output of 285hp and a whopping 410lb-ft of torque.

To ensure cool intake air on hot days, and lower the risk of detonation, Lincoln engineers provided for a second intake path that drew air directly from the grille. This cool-air path came into play when a thermostatic valve in the air cleaner horn opened past a certain point, closing the under-hood source and admitting cool air from the front of the car. These engines were used on the elegant Continental Mark II and all other Lincoln models. As a side note, Lincolns switched from a 6- to a 12-volt electrical system in 1956, in step with most other domestic makes. This provided more cranking power to start the higher compression engine and to run the rapidly proliferating list of power accessories on mid- and high-end models.

Despite the jump in power in 1956, Lincoln engineers realized that they still had not reached the horsepower ceiling of their excellent V-8. So, they tweaked it still further in 1957. Changes included raising the compression ratio to an even 10.0:1 through the use of domed pistons and shrinking the combustion chamber.

The distributor was replaced with a unit that allowed more spark advance, and carburetor capacity was raised with larger float bowls. These changes resulted in 300hp from the same 368ci displacement. But the jumps in horsepower and displacement had just begun.

With a massively longer, larger, heavier car in the showrooms for 1958, a completely new 430ci engine began powering all Lincoln models. This was the first "divisional" engine and was known as the "MEL" engine, since it was shared by Mercury, Edsel, and Lincoln. The MEL, although based on the design principles of the 1952 V-8, was part of the "FE" series of big-block engines from Ford. The MEL was also a 90deg, pushrod V-8, but it had a more massive, fully webbed block, true wedge-shaped combustion chambers, and a 4.29x3.7in bore and stroke. It used flat-surfaced heads and a block milled 10deg shorter on the inboard sides of the cylinder banks than on the outside. When the heads were bolted on, the combustion chamber wedge was created by the disparity in the height of one side of the deck versus the other. Intake and exhaust manifolds were huge in cross-section, and the crank was much beefier than in the 368ci engine.

The MEL, as used in Lincolns, developed 375bhp and a gigantic 490lb-ft of torque. Powered by these engines, the 4800lb 1958 Lincolns, with their brick-like aerodynamics, could run from 0 to 60mph in less than ten seconds, a remarkable accomplishment. If anything, these engines were too powerful for the kind of sedate drivers who traditionally bought Lincolns. For 1959, compression was lowered to 10.0:1 (from 10.5:1), a two-barrel carburetor replaced the four-barrel unit, and horsepower retreated to 350bhp.

The monstrous 1958, '59, and '60 Lincolns were made at the Wixom assembly plant alongside Ford Thunderbirds and featured the same sort of large scale unibody construction. They were the biggest cars up to that time to use a frameless build. The process was not altogether successful, and these cars had a reputation for developing leaks, rattles, and rust. Although an air suspension was seriously considered for the 1958 Lincolns, with air bags replacing the rear coil springs, it would take just about two decades for it to become a reality.

Nineteen sixty-one saw an all-new Lincoln: the four-door sedan and convertible Continental. This vehicle also had unibody construction and was built in the Wixom plant, alongside the Thunderbird, because they shared a common cowl structure. The MEL engine continued as the powerplant of the new Continental; but, with further detuning, it now produced

300bhp and delivered 12 to 14mpg. This engine package continued through the 1965 model year.

In 1966, a restyle of the original slab-sided Continental seemed a good time for a new motor package. The car was growing larger again, and engineers felt it could benefit from more power to be competitive with the high-compression, higher-revving engines from Cadillac and Chrysler. The enlarged MEL had a bore and stroke of 4.38x3.83in for a displacement of 462ci. This larger engine was rated at 340hp and 485lb-ft of torque. Used in all Lincoln vehicles, the larger MEL was linked to an improved Twin-Range Turbo Drive automatic transmission.

With concerns for fuel economy mounting again, a new engine design, the "385-series," was introduced for Lincoln. Producing a healthy 365hp, the engine had power, flexibility, and reasonable economy.

The 385, in almost exactly this same form, continued on as the sole Lincoln powerplant until 1977, when the Versailles was introduced. The Versailles used Ford's corporate 351 small-block V-8; cars destined for California or high-altitude areas like Denver were equipped with the 302 V-8.

Meanwhile, a 400ci engine became available as an optional powerplant. Big engines were going out of favor in this era of gas shortages and oil embargoes.

In 1980, the era of downsizing engulfed Lincoln bodies, and the engines' sizes were trimmed to match. The standard engine for the whole model line became the Ford 302 V-8, with the 351W available as a more powerful option on the Mark and Continental. The 302 was equipped with an early form of electronic fuel injection (EFI) and developed 129hp while the 351W was good for 140hp. As the trend toward downsizing continued, the 1981 model year saw the 302 as the only engine available for Lincoln, in 130bhp trim.

In 1984, you might say that the new Continental Mark VII was given only half a traditional Lincoln engine, an I-6. But here was an unusual engine package—a 149ci turbo-diesel sourced from BMW. With a 3.15x3.19in bore and stroke, this resident alien churned out 115hp in a car that weighed 3600lb. It was not a marriage made in heaven. This optional engine continued on into the 1985 model year but was quickly dropped from availability due to abysmal sales.

Improvements in EFI and engine management allowed the 302 V-8s used in Lincoln cars to increase in horsepower as the decade rumbled on. Ford was quickly becoming a world leader in automotive electronics, and its EEC (Electronic Engine Control) became one

This cutaway of the 4.6 dohc clearly shows the hollow camshafts, which are made by pressing the hard steel cam lobes onto the shafts which are cast from an aluminum power alloy. The cam lobes then contact roller rockers, generating the minimum of slope in the valve train. *Credit: Ford Motor Company*

of the best engine management systems available.

By 1988, the standard 302 was producing 150hp, and the high output version exclusive to the sporty Mark VII LSC was rated at a healthy 225bhp. Also in 1988, the debut of a new Continental based on the Taurus/Sable platform saw the introduction of the first gasoline V-6 into the Lincoln product line, the 3.8ltr first used on the Taurus and Sable. This 232ci, 90deg V-6 engine had a bore and stroke of 3.81x3.39in. Due to modern computer-aided design and manufacturing techniques, advanced metallurgy, and the accumulated

experience of decades of making engines, the 3.8ltr produced 140hp, just ten less than the 302 V-8. In 1989, sequential multi-port fuel injection was added to the 3.8, and its torque peak was increased. These changes made the engine more driveable, but the horsepower rating remained at 140bhp.

In 1991, Lincoln took a major step forward in engine technology when the recently introduced third-generation Town Car got the superb new 190hp, 4.6ltr sohc modular V-8. The modular engine is part of a new Ford philosophy of producing a family of engines, all with identical bore spacing and all machined on the same assembly lines whether they are V-8, in-line 4, V-6, or whatever.

The 4.6ltr sohc engine represents a highly evolved V-8 concept, but it is just the beginning. In 1993, Lincoln introduced its ultimate personal luxury car, the Continental Mark VIII with a 32-valve, dohc version of the 4.6ltr engine that is truly exotic and certainly is the most advanced V-8 produced domestically, including the Cadillac Northstar system.

The dohc 4.6ltr V-8 represents the culmination of more than sixty years of Ford Motor Company experience in building V-8 engines. It is the first four-valves-per-cylinder, dohc V-8 to be mass produced by Lincoln and the make's first all-aluminum V-8. In the Lincoln Mark VIII, this engine is rated at 280hp at 5500rpm and 285lb-ft of torque at 4500rpm, about 33 percent more power than its cast-iron sohc brother. Ninety-five percent of peak torque is available from 2000 to 5750rpm, making a flexible engine and one with quick acceleration response.

The brake-specific fuel consumption of the aluminum dohc 4.6 V-8 is 3 to 6 percent better than Japanese competitors—meaning Lexus and Infinity—and roughly 7 percent better than the Mark VII's 5ltr HO pushrod engine.

The two major differences between this engine and the iron sohc 4.6ltr are: the 32-valve, dohc aluminum cylinder heads and aluminum block construction. Bore and stroke are identical at 90.2x90.0mm, on 100mm bore centers. The gravity cast-aluminum block uses pressed-in iron cylinder liners with a 2.3mm wall thickness.

The aluminum block itself has stiff, deep-skirt construction, with extra metal around the bottom of the block to increase structural strength and reduce noise, vibration, and harshness (NVH). The dohc uses six bolts on each of five main bearing caps—four vertical bolts and two horizontal cross-bolts to maintain crank straightness and better distribute loads across the block. An aluminum alloy front cover is a structural part of the engine. It seals the camshaft drive chains and serves as a mounting point for the air conditioning compressor, power steering pump, and a 120amp alternator.

The block is a "dry-valley" design, because there are no camshafts, tappets, or pushrods in the space between the cylinder banks to require lubrication. This space is used for a clever inverted plenum intake manifold, which helps to reduce the overall height of the engine but maintains proper runner length for the intake system.

Connecting rods for this engine are unique in that they are made from powdered metal in one piece and then "cracked" across the big ends. When they are re-assembled around the crankshaft, the metal grain of the cracked halves mates better than two machined surfaces and provides a slip-free joint when torqued to the correct clamping force.

Pistons are slightly dished. They are made of aluminum alloy in a short-skirt design, weigh 354 grams each, and have a three-ring design—one oil and two compression. The engine's crankshaft is nodular iron. The induction system uses two progressive 55mm throttle plates, leading into the inverted plenum and then into sixteen tubular intake runners, each of which feeds an individual intake valve. Each cylinder uses a single fuel injector. The primary ports are designed to generate an intense swirl of the intake charge for good burn, low emissions, and strong low-speed torque.

The sixteen intake runners constitute a primary and secondary system of eight runners each, with the secondaries closed off until about 3200rpm, at which point they open to increase high-speed airflow. The port-throttle arrangement not only enhances torque but also controls the combustion sequence by gradually changing the high-swirl into a tumbling of the air/fuel mixture at higher rpm.

The aluminum heads in the engine use two 37mm intake valves and two 30mm exhaust valves per cylinder, rather than the single 44.5mm intake and 34mm exhaust valves of the sohc version. The four-valve heads deliver 40 percent more intake and 35 percent more exhaust area, especially at higher rpm. The quad cams are spun by a "silent" chain. There are four chains and four tensioners in the cam drive system. Each intake valve has a separate cam profile to match the low- and high-speed needs of the engine, but both develop a 10mm lift. Exhaust valves work in unison. Camshafts are hollow tubes of aluminum with the lobes pressed on and secured with locating tabs. Exhaust manifolds are fabricated from stainless steel and dump into two separate palladium and rhodium, three-way catalytic converters.

This engine uses distributorless ignition, fired by two coils located at the front of the engine. Controlled by Ford's EEC-IV computer, the engine not only monitors its own performance but communicates with the automatic transmission to control gear shift points, torque converter lock-up, and spark retardation across the gear change to reduce shift-shock under heavy acceleration. The dohc 4.6 idles at 575rpm and has a Hardware Limited Operation Strategy, or limp-home

Same engine, same angle, but zoom out. This magnificent motor was developed to be powerful and quiet, and to have superior flexibility under varied driving conditions. A group of powertrain and other engineers came together to design and build this engine, and the results are world-class. *Credit: Ford Motor Company*

mode in case of EEC system failure.

All power accessories mount directly to the front of the engine and are driven by a single, long, grooved serpentine belt. This design reduces cost, weight, and assembly time by eliminating all mounting brackets. It also improves serviceability by placing all these components at the front of the engine compartment.

The 4.6 dohc is matched to Ford's 4R70W electronic transmission in the Mark VIII. The 4R70W has a 2.84:1 gear in first, a 1.56:1 in second, 1:1 in third, and an overdrive ratio of 0.70:1 in fourth.

This magnificent motor is built alongside the sohc version at Ford's engine plant in Romeo, Michigan, north of Detroit. It is built on a precision assembly line 1600ft long that is capable of ultimately producing 700,000 engines per year. Ford estimates that 40,000 to 50,000 4.6 dohc engines will be constructed annually.

Powered by the modular engines, both sohc and dohc versions, Lincoln products approach the twenty-first century with a new dedication to precision that is thoroughly in keeping with the cars' origins in the 1920s with old Henry Leland, the master of precision. It is a fitting legacy.

Chapter 7

Presidential Lincolns, Lincoln Limousines, and Stretched Lincolns

It was a bright, sunny day in Dallas, Texas, a warm day, for the end of November. Slowly, the parade wound its way through the streets, past the cheering crowds, past the occasional sour face.

Then, shots rang out and sent the motorcade rushing for safety, the crowds scattering. Exactly how many shots, who fired them, and from whence they came may never be known, but what is known is that John Fitzgerald Kennedy, the charismatic thirty-fifth president of the United States, died from wounds suffered during the gunfire that occurred on November 22, 1963. He was riding in a custom-built presidential Lincoln limousine at the time of his assassination.

In an instant, that Lincoln Continental became the most famous car in history, viewed on film and tape uncountable times during the 1960s and again over the following decades. The image of that Lincoln has become part of our national mythology, branded on the soul of a nation like no other.

In a tragic, mournful way, that vehicle illustrates an important point about Lincoln cars. They have been the leading choice for state vehicles in the United States and many other countries since before World War II. The other countries that use them are mostly our direct allies, although President Nixon presented a Continental Town Car to Soviet First Secretary and later President Leonid Brezhnev as a token of good will in 1973. How often Brezhnev used the car or what became of it is not currently known. But, in another fifteen years, the Communist oligarchy was gone. That's the power of a Lincoln!

American presidents have always taken a liking to Lincolns, perhaps because the car is named after one of their own. While some US presidents have preferred the competition, Cadillac, including Mustang fan Bill Clinton, a majority of first families have driven to and from the White House in Lincoln motorcars of one sort or another.

This relationship may have begun in the mid-1920s, when the White House ordered a Lincoln L Phaeton for President Calvin Coolidge, through Ralph Roberts of LeBaron, the custom coachbuilders. Old "Silent Cal," supposedly took delivery of his Lincoln L and used it through the duration of his administration, passing the car to Herbert Hoover just in time for the great stock market crash of 1929. Records for this car are elusive, and it may have been only a loaner from Lincoln to the White House for a state visit by British Prime Minister Lloyd George in 1923. Hoover, the thirty-first president of the United States, presided over the beginning of the Great Depression and couldn't afford to buy a new car for the White House, so he seems to have kept Coolidge's Lincoln L and used it as a parade and touring car.

Along with a "New Deal," Franklin Delano Roosevelt's election brought several new cars into the White House motor pool. A 1939 Lincoln convertible with brown leather seats became one of the best known cars in the United States, due to the enormity of Roosevelt's wartime exposure. It was also a more modified vehicle than any that had come before it. With the threat of real wartime enemies on all sides, this Lincoln, known as the "Sunshine Special," was built on a 161in wheelbase and had 1in-thick bulletproof glass on all sides. It had armor plates in the doors and fenders. A loud, police-type siren on the left front side was stamped "Double Tone Long Roll Siren/Made by Federal Electric Co., Chicago, Ill." There was a special compartment for Thompson submachine guns, two foot plates at the rear of the Sunshine Special for Secret Service Agents, and an antenna mount for a two-way radio.

The vehicle was 245in long, 76.5in wide, and weighed 9300lb compared to other customs built on the same wheelbase that weighed under 6,000lb. De-

The royal parasol is proudly displayed by the Queen Mum as she and King George IV tour the United States and Canada in 1939. The Lincoln is a 1939 seven-passenger phaeton, specially outfitted for the royal couple. This vehicle was then displayed at the Henry Ford Museum in Dearborn, Michigan. It was brought out of retirement for Queen Elizabeth's 1959 visit to Canada. *Credit: Ford Motor Company*

spite its extra weight, the Sunshine Special used a stock 150hp Lincoln V-12 engine and three-speed transmission. One of the most durable of White House cars, the Sunshine Special accompanied Roosevelt on many wartime trips, including conferences in Malta, Casablanca, Yalta, and Teheran.

Two or more four-door sedans were also part of the presidential motor pool for winter assignments and inclement weather days in Washington, D.C. In Roosevelt's case, these were also Lincolns. The longest lasting were a pair of 1942 limousines that were substantially updated by the Lincoln factory in 1946.

After Roosevelt's death in 1945, Harry Truman became the thirty-third president of the United States and continued using the Sunshine Special for state functions, including his infamous reelection campaign of 1948. Truman and the Sunshine Special retired together in 1950, although Truman got a few rides in the new presidential car, delivered for Republican President-elect Dwight Eisenhower.

This new vehicle, also a Lincoln, was based on the 1950 Cosmopolitan convertible, styled by Raymond Dietrich and modified at his shop in Grand Rapids, Michigan. It was glossy black with chrome trim and had black-and-red leather inside, with fold-down jump seats to accommodate extra passengers. This car was

The "Sunshine Special" of FDR meets its replacement, the "Bubble Top" of Harry Truman, outside the White House. Major Cunningham of the Secret Service bids the Sunshine Special a sad farewell. *Credit: Henry Ford Museum and Greenfield Village*

called the "Bubble Top" after the heavy Plexiglas hemisphere that formed the rear of the roof, so people could see Ike and his guests on crowded parade routes. There were stanchions for US flags on the front bumpers, twin spotlights at the A-pillars, and a special platform for the Secret Service agents to stand on. Although a heavy-duty Hydra-Matic automatic transmission was used, the engine was the stock L-head, 337ci V-8. This car weighed 5000lb and was 262in long.

This Bubble Top Cosmopolitan put in as much service as the Sunshine Special had before it. Four presidents rode in it and so did numerous other dignitaries. Truman, Eisenhower, Kennedy, and Lyndon B. Johnson all used the car at one time or another, but by the time Kennedy was in office, the Bubble Top had become a back-up vehicle with the newer 1961 Conti-

A side view of the Bubble Top. Although the car was built for and used first by President Harry Truman, its bubble top was constructed and installed in 1954 at the request of President Eisenhower. *Credit: Ford Motor Company*

nental as the lead presidential car.

The Kennedy limousine, made by coachbuilders Hess & Eisenhardt, not Lincoln, was based on the unibody of a 1961 Continental but was almost completely hand-built. It was nearly 3ft longer than the production Continental and weighed 3800lb more than stock.

Bill Hess, former owner of Hess & Eisenhardt said, "We built that car from scratch. I was in charge of the engineering project. We cooperated with the Secret Service as to specifications and then, in turn, worked with the entire Ford and Lincoln engineering staff as liaison for technical assistance. We took their largest chassis and lengthened that, but with very close guidance from Lin-

coln, because they owned the car and they were going to take care of it. We called it X-100, and it carried that name through its life at the White House and still carries that name at the Henry Ford Museum. Kennedy's assassination put a halt to the open parade vehicle. The X-100 was brought back to our Cincinnati plant and through many negotiations in Washington with the War Department (*sic*) and many security agencies, it was converted into a stationary bubble-top limousine for President Johnson. And, of course, the rear is the first piece of molded bullet-resisting glass in the world. And it extended from the deck up to the hinge pillar, and from that point forward there were glass panels in the roof."

Harry Truman pays a presidential visit to Los Angeles in June 1948. The car he's riding in appears to be a stock Lincoln convertible; however, the president's car is followed by what is clearly one of the Secret Service Lincolns with running boards and more. As a further item of interest, both cars carry the same license plate number, 1509. *Credit: Henry Ford Museum and Greenfield Village*

The X-100's equipment included a large number of safety and security features: two radiotelephones and other communications gear, heavy armoring, including the floor pan and tires, separate front and rear air conditioning, a presidential rear seat that could be raised 10in to allow the crowd a better view, and special nonglare lights to illuminate the president on dark days or night parades. There were three see-through removable roofs of different design, and each had enough headroom to allow the president to wear a top hat, if he so desired.

After the Kennedy assassination, the car was completely refurbished and used by Lyndon Baines Johnson, the thirty-sixth president of the United States. You have to wonder if it gave him the willies, Texas machismo or not, to sit in the back seat of that car and hear the tumult of the crowds.

Along with the Sunshine Special and the Bubble-Top, the X-100 now resides in the Henry Ford Museum in Dearborn, Michigan, keeping an epic corner of American history carefully to itself.

Richard Nixon, whatever else his flaws, would not ride in anything but a Lincoln. Even years after he left the presidency, Nixon insisted on Lincoln Town Cars as his preferred mode of transportation, and always chauffeured.

When Nixon was in the White House, he had the most lavish and fully equipped presidential limousine ever built custom-made for him in 1969. This vehicle probably began as a 1967-1968 Continental limo and was then refitted by Lehmann-Peterson. Perhaps some can see the man's paranoia at work in a car with over two tons of armor plating, including rubber-edged steel discs in the wheels, so that the car could still be driven up to

Here the president waves to the crowd during a 1950 parade in Washington, D.C. This looks like the bubble top car that Ike had crafted from Truman's parade Lincoln. *Credit: Henry Ford Museum and Greenfield Village*

According to Lincoln Public Relations this is, "The first of a fleet of nine custom Lincoln Cosmopolitan Limousines and one seven-passenger convertible which have been delivered to the White House for President Truman's use."

The passenger compartment is separated from the driver's compartment by an electrically controlled glass partition. Fixtures in the passenger section are gold-plated. *Credit: Ford Motor Company*

50mph even with all four tires shot to ribbons. Nixon's limo was 258.3in long, with a wheelbase of 160in.

Beginning with the 1969 Lincoln parade car, presidential limousines became more sophisticated, heavier, and vastly more expensive. Security and armoring were increased, as were onboard communications and other electronic systems. Also beginning with the 1969 car, exact details of presidential cars became highly classified. Although the true figures are not for public release, that presidential Lincoln cost in excess of half a million

dollars (1969 dollars!) and weighed just under six tons. Forget fuel mileage.

To give presidential parades a more consistent look, the Secret Service ordered two other Lincolns to run behind the presidential car, or for use by foreign royals or heads of state while in the United States. They were extensively modified 1968 Continentals with running boards on either side, a platform at the rear for agents to stand on, and other security hardware.

To replace the aging 1961 parade car, a new Lin-

For 1959, this Lincoln Continental Mark IV Limousine offered a special padded, landau-type roof extending back over the rear with a small formal window. The car was available only in black. A retracting, curved-glass partition separates the chauffeur from his passengers and can be operated from either front or rear seats. *Credit: Ford Motor Company*

coln Town Sedan limo went into White House service in 1972. Both Richard Nixon and Jimmy Carter used this car as an alternate vehicle. Gerald Ford also used the 1972 car during his campaign of 1976.

During the middle and late 1970s, more Lincolns were added to the White House motor pool. In 1974, two Sand Beige sedans were purchased. One was a presidential back-up car for occasional or casual use, the other for Vice President Rockefeller. In 1977, a silver sedan became the new presidential second car, and the VP took delivery of a new Lincoln sedan in navy blue. These cars shared specifications with the 1972 vehicle.

Perhaps due to his anti-Washington stance, Ronald Reagan employed Cadillac limos as presidential cars during his two terms in office, but George Bush switched back to the more traditional Lincoln. Just as Bush commissioned a new fleet of 747s as his Air Force One aircraft, he also had completely new limos built for his tenure in office. Designed by a highly secretive group of engineers at Ford's Advanced Vehicle Development center, the 1989 presidential limo represented the ultimate in security measures, two-way communications, and advanced electronic features—including anti-jamming radios, high speed data links, and military-style lo-

cation transponders. It is rumored that O'Gara-Hess & Eisenhardt coachbuilders required nearly a year to complete the complex steel and Nomex armoring that enveloped the passenger compartment on all sides.

President Bill Clinton sought out Cadillac style for his parade limos, details of which are closely held by the Secret Service and are publicly unavailable.

US presidents were not the only ones privileged to ride in Lincoln limousines. Even this humble author has had the pleasure, on occasion, of luxuriating in the 1990 series Town Car, the most popular stretched limo in history, and perhaps the best. From the earliest days of Lincoln bodies, a limousine spin-off has always been part of the Lincoln legacy. That's just as true today, perhaps more so, than it was in 1930s.

From the earliest days of Lincoln production, the old Model L Lincolns were a favorite for fitment with a limousine body. Whether it was by Brunn, Dietrich, Murray, or LeBaron, all the United States' best coachbuilders produced Lincoln limousines with elongated bodies on the long wheelbase version of the Model L and other early Lincoln chassis.

With the demise of coachbuilding and the Lincoln Division's turn to servicing the great upper-middle

Holy limo! This Lincoln Continental Executive Limousine was specially constructed for the visit of Pope Paul VI to New York City. Based on a 1964 Continental, this limo is a 34in stretch from the original and includes an elevated seat for the Pope, a public address and lighting system, and running boards for security personnel. The vehicle also has a detachable top, which is not shown in this picture. *Credit: Ford Motor Company*

Long, lean, and elegant, this 1967 Lincoln Continental limousine was modified by Lehmann-Peterson of Chicago. It represents advances in styling, safety, privacy, and comfort from its predecessors. This limo has a wheelbase of 160in, compared to the stock dimension of 125in. It sold for $17,000 to $18,000. *Credit: Ford Motor Company*

class, limousines went out of style for a time, except for those delivered to exclusive customers such as American presidents and foreign heads of state. But in the 1960s, despite the bad associations connected with the Kennedy X-100, custom body firms realized that the 1961 Continental made a superb looking limousine, and a trend began. Hess & Eisenhardt of Cincinnati and Lehmann-Peterson of Chicago both developed "executive" limousines based on the Continental.

In 1963, Lehmann-Peterson offered its Executive Limousine in conjunction with Lincoln. These cars could be ordered through Lincoln dealers and carried Ford model number 53A. These vehicles retained their two-year, 24,000-mile factory warranty, despite extensive modifications to the body and chassis. Setting the stage for many successors that came later, this conversion used a 36in plug placed into the body just behind the B-pillar. The completed conversion had a wheelbase

Left, inside this 1966 Lincoln Executive Limousine are the kind of thick plush carpets, pretty wood veneer, heavy chrome plating, and other luxury elements that we expect in a limo. Still, this interior looks barren compared to the latest limos with their wet bars and TVs. *Credit: Ford Motor Company*

Next page, President Kennedy and staff crowd into a 1961 Continental on a presidential trip. The license plate at the rear of this car seems to indicate that it was sourced from a local dealership. Imagine how easy it would be to sell this car to a Democrat. *Credit: Henry Ford Museum and Greenfield Village*

The X-100, that special custom Continental presidential limousine built by Hess & Eisenhardt of Cincinnati, Ohio. Today this car is prominently displayed at the Henry Ford Museum and Greenfield Village in Dearborn, Michigan. The X-100 was used by Presidents Kennedy and Johnson, and then retired. *Credit: Henry Ford Museum and Greenfield Village*

of 159in and an overall length of 249in, compared to the 123in wheelbase and 213in length of the stock Continental. Inside was a luxurious atmosphere suited to captains of industry and show business moguls. Added features included mouton carpeting, tuck-and-roll leather seating areas, a miniwet bar, a drop-leaf table and secretary's desk, television, AM-FM stereo radio, and a power window in the back of the front seat to isolate the chauffeur. Overall, this limo conversion weighed 5540lb and sold for $13,500.

In 1964, Lincoln embraced this conversion even more, buying one of its own for testing purposes. The '64 version of the Lehmann-Peterson Executive was 2in shorter than the first model, for better torsional rigidity, weighed 100lb more, and sold for $15,153. While only two of these vehicles were sold in 1963, the '64 offering was wildly popular in comparison with fifteen units sold. By 1965, this figure would jump to eighty-five, with the package now available in several colors besides the basic black and white. Sales then diminished slightly, down to fifty-six in 1968.

Carron & Company of Inkster, Michigan, just outside Dearborn, performed a unique Continental stretch in 1969 for "The Great One," Jackie Gleason. With elegantly concealed headlamps, raised roof, and a greenhouse-sized sunroof above the whole passenger compartment, this was one of the more interesting Lincoln limo conversions. Fitting for a TV star of the first magnitude, Gleason's car is rumored to have cost $65,000. A price The Great One could easily afford. Somehow, that price tag doesn't seem so outlandish today, when many upscale cars have comparable MSRPs.

In 1971, the Andy Hotten Company jumped into the Lincoln limo market with a choice of stretches: 12in or 24in. With an enlarged, formal roof, a compact backlight, and some Mark III styling cues, such as the tire bump on the trunk lid, these were pretty and practical Lincoln conversions.

As the 1980s clanked into the 1990s, more Lincoln stretched limos were being built than ever before. The 1990 Town Car provided an excellent platform for limo conversions, since it began as one of the largest cars left

in the domestic market and was a superbly quiet riding automobile in stock trim. A slew of specialty companies, as well as the more established coachbuilders, turned out stretched Town Cars with quality and panel-fits ranging from exquisite to just plain sad. One of the best Lincoln limousine converters in the United States in the mid-1990s is American Custom Coachworks of Beverly Hills. American Custom has been

around, under family ownership, since the 1950s. The current president, Jay Meyers, aims to make owning a limo just like owning any other car, with dealerships in most major cities and local service outlets. "We are continuing to pioneer the idea of customer service by helping buyers with everything from shopping for limousine loans and leases to convenient maintenance and servicing," Meyers said.

To get a feel for the Lincoln limo conversion business in the 1990s, we spoke with American Custom's sales manager, Virgil Budnic, and national service manager, Bob Jones. Budnic spoke of the growth of interest in Lincoln limos over the past fifteen years. He told us that fifteen years ago, nearly all the limos built for commercial use were Cadillacs. But then, Cadillac brought out its infamous V-8-6-4 engine and the 4.1ltr power-

This 60in stretch St. Tropez limo from American Custom Coachworks is a popular private limo based on the durable 1990s series Town Car platform. It's interesting to note how the proportions of the Town Car, especially the long rear overhang, allow for stretching the car without destroying its visual integrity. *Credit: American Custom Coachworks*

plant, neither of which was powerful enough to pull a stretched limo and its contents. As a result, the field of coachbuilders who specialize in stretched limos began turning to Lincoln. Now, they "cut" fifteen Lincolns to every Cadillac, just the reverse of the situation two decades ago.

And recently, to no one's surprise, the federal government has begun to monitor the limo conversion business closely. In the past, Budnic said, anyone could be a coachbuilder if they had a garage and a cutting torch. Now Ford and GM have programs designed to ensure the quality of the work done by coachbuilders and the safety of the occupants of the limo. Ford calls its program QVM, for Quality Vehicle Modifier. To be certified in this program, as American Custom Coach-

works is, requires following strict rules laid down by the OEM, and crash testing a fully complete vehicle, often a quarter-million-dollar prototype. And the National Highway Traffic Safety Administration (NHTSA) gets in the act too, requiring certain safety standards and monitoring the crash test. Consequently, the number of coachbuilders doing limo conversions has shrunk from forty to about fifteen in the past ten years.

To make a stretched Lincoln, in the manner of ACC, you first need a Lincoln, probably a Town Car, with the heavy-duty "418" coachbuilder package on it (heavy-duty shocks, springs, and sway bars, HD alternator, oil and transmission coolers, and so on). Then you have this car delivered to your factory where it is gutted and extra soundproofing material is added.

A 68in stretched Lincoln Town Car based limo is identified by the three "opera light" bars on the B- and C-pillars. *Credit: American Custom Coachworks*

Inside the 68in stretch St. Tropez limo, everything is first class materials—fine wood veneers, supple leather, and deep pile carpeting. There's also a wet bar, a TV, and stereo and storage compartments for hiding valuables while you are at dinner or at a concert. *Credit: American Custom Coachworks*

Then the car is attached to a precision jig and cut behind the B-pillar with a "cold" torch. In the past, saws were used for the cutting job, but they left the car's sheet metal red hot, and the cut car would have to sit for two days while it cooled enough to be worked on.

Then, with the support beams below the floor already in place, the jig is pulled apart to whatever length of stretch is required— 60in, 68in, 90in, 100in. Next, plugs made from 12-, 14-, and 16-gauge steel are welded into place, and the interior work begins. The plugs for the floor, side panels, and roof, along with virtually everything else that goes into the limos (cabinetry, fittings, trim, moldings, wiring harnesses, and so on), are all made by American Custom Coachworks in its Arkansas factory. The company does its own upholstery of the Lincoln limo's front J seat as well.

A stretched rear-drive Town Car also needs a stretched drive shaft. For the smaller limos, a two-piece is sufficient; for the longer cars, a three-piece drive shaft is necessary. Getting the stretched drive shaft to work

Left, going up! This 90in stretch can be identified by the four "opera lights" on its B- and C-pillars. Most impressive about this conversion is the absolute straightness of the roof, trim lines, and rocker panels. Despite massive conversion efforts, this vehicle looks like it just came from the Lincoln factory. *Credit: American Custom Coachworks*

properly can be a chore. Says Bob Jones, "The biggest problem you have is maintaining them. We have had our own problems with drive shafts out of balance. You get an awful vibration in the back and hear this thing clunking. It was either a faulty way it was put on, the yoke wasn't right, or it's not loaded to the frame right and you're hitting one of the cross-members."

Jones has also instituted "teams" at the ACC factory so that each group of artisans and craftspeople sign off on their duties and pass the car-in-progress along to the next group. This system helps them keep quality standards high.

In ACC's St. Tropez series of stretched Lincolns, special recommended equipment includes color TV, separate rear air conditioning and heating control, electric chauffeur divider window (heavily soundproofed), illuminated decanter storage and ice compartment, dual battery system, overhead lighting and control, intercom, trash chute, side console cabinet, and so on. The short list of options includes a VCR, gold trim package, and a custom front grille.

Surprisingly, the price for one of these elegant mile-long Lincolns runs from the low $50s to high $60s, competitive with a Lexus LS400, Infiniti Q45, several Mercedes, and many other luxury competitors. Sounds like a heck of a deal.

What the Lincoln limo faces in the future is a question without an answer. None of the major coachbuilders is really prepared for alternative fuels or electric power. But for the moment, the status quo seems more than adequate. Several reputable shops are turning out a steady supply of stretched Lincolns for private, corporate, and commercial use, and business seems to be booming.

Although the 1990-1993 recession hurt sales a bit, Virgil Budnic mentioned the opening markets of Singapore, China, and surprisingly, Russia, where President Boris Yeltsen recently bought an ACC stretched Lincoln limo for his own use. Ah, the joys of democracy!

The dominance of Lincoln in the limousine field is probably safe for the present. As I was leaving American Custom Coachworks, they showed me Lincoln and Cadillac limos side by side. The Cadillac had a small trunk, less usable interior space, and a deep dashboard that took wheelbase inches away from the rear cabin. Sorry, Caddy. Bill Clinton or no, the Lincoln, named after a US president, is still America's first choice for limousine service and affairs of State.

Left, inside the 90in stretched Town Car is a world of luxury and comfort. The popular "J" seat adds passenger room while disguising the drive-line hump. Color TV, cell phone, and cassette stereo, along with moonroof and separate AC controls, make this a superb way to get from here to there. *Credit: American Custom Coachworks*

Darned near as long as a Pullman car, this 100in super-stretch St. Tropez Town Car is known as the "Celebrity Edition," because you have to be very wealthy to own one, or have plenty of room on your credit card for a rental. The entire prom of a small town could fit in this ultra stretch. Steer a supertanker, or drive one of these, the choice is yours. *Credit: American Custom Coachworks*

The inside of the super-stretch St. Tropez contains two TVs, an enormous "J" seat, recessed mood lighting, cut crystal bottles in a hand-built, mirrored liquor cabinet, and more amenities than most of us can imagine. Precise fit and finish and a superior design sense make the St. Tropez line some of the best limo conversions this author has ever experienced. *Credit: American Custom Coachworks*

Right top and bottom, two pages from the service manual written by American Custom Coachworks show that making a stretched limo is not a job for the shade-tree mechanic. Precision and craftsmanship mean everything in a business that works to satisfy the toughest customer in the car business, the limo buyer or renter. *Credit: American Custom Coachworks*

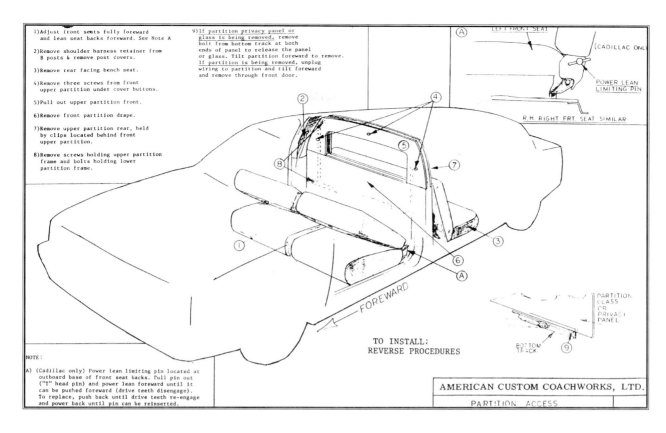

1) Adjust front seats fully foreward and lean seat backs foreward. See Note A

2) Remove shoulder harness retainer from B posts & remove post covers.

3) Remove rear facing bench seat.

4) Remove three screws from front upper partition under cover buttons.

5) Pull out upper partition front.

6) Remove front partition drape.

7) Remove upper partition rear, held by clips located behind front upper partition.

8) Remove screws holding upper partition frame and bolts holding lower partition frame.

9) If partition privacy panel or glass is being removed, remove bolt from bottom track at both ends of panel to release the panel or glass. Tilt partition foreward to remove. If partition is being removed, unplug wiring to partition and tilt foreward and remove through front door.

LEFT FRONT SEAT

(CADILLAC ONLY)

POWER LEAN LIMITING PIN

R.H. RIGHT FRT. SEAT SIMILAR

FOREWARD

PARTITION GLASS OR PRIVACY PANEL

BOTTOM TRACK

TO INSTALL:
REVERSE PROCEDURES

NOTE:

A) (Cadillac only) Power lean limiting pin located at outboard base of front seat backs. Pull pin out ("T" head pin) and power lean forward until it can be pushed foreward (drive teeth disengage). To replace, push back until drive teeth re-engage and power back until pin can be reinserted.

AMERICAN CUSTOM COACHWORKS, LTD.

PARTITION ACCESS

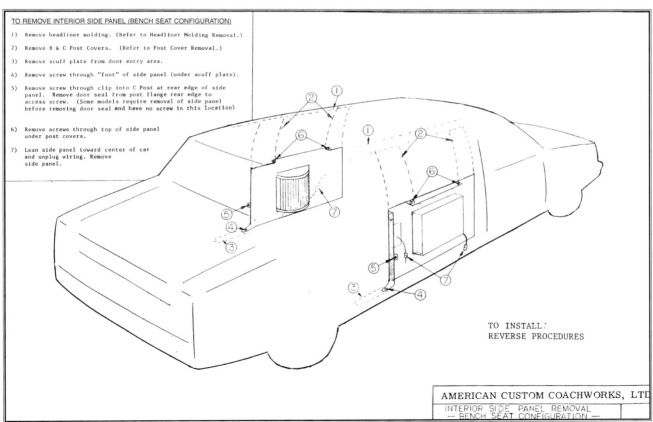

TO REMOVE INTERIOR SIDE PANEL (BENCH SEAT CONFIGURATION)

1) Remove headliner molding. (Refer to Headliner Molding Removal.)

2) Remove B & C Post Covers. (Refer to Post Cover Removal.)

3) Remove scuff plate from door entry area.

4) Remove screw through "foot" of side panel (under scuff plate).

5) Remove screw through clip into C Post at rear edge of side panel. Remove door seal from post flange rear edge to access screw. (Some models require removal of side panel before removing door seal and have no screw in this location)

6) Remove screws through top of side panel under post covers.

7) Lean side panel toward center of car and unplug wiring. Remove side panel.

TO INSTALL:
REVERSE PROCEDURES

AMERICAN CUSTOM COACHWORKS, LTD

INTERIOR SIDE PANEL REMOVAL
— BENCH SEAT CONFIGURATION —

Chapter 8

Lincoln In Competition

It might seem strange that a car so well known for comfort, luxury, and prestige should have a racing history too. In the case of the Lincoln, it is a curious history, indeed. Even more curious is the fact that the Lincolns came home winners, dominating their competitors.

Surprisingly, there is a precedent, you might even say a tradition, of luxury cars at speed.

Rolls-Royce originally came to prominence through its success in motor races, driven by no less a person than the honorable C.S. Rolls himself. Other

A busy Lincoln pit crew prepares one of the cars for another grueling day of racing at the Carrera Panamericana. Lincoln's domination of this on-road race was a surprise to everyone. *Credit: Henry Ford Museum and Greenfield Village; Photographer: Mackenzie*

Bill Stroppe addresses the drivers and crews in the Lincoln HQ at a Carrera Panamericana. Contrast the garb worn by the drivers with today's helmets, gloves, and driving suits!

makes known for their upper-class connections, such as Mercedes, Bentley, Duesenberg, Auburn, and certainly Bugatti, made enviable racing records for themselves.

Lincolns were never meant to race, it's true, but the Carrera Panamericana was not your average Sunday race, either. In the 1950s, there was an exciting tradition of on-road enduros with the finest of competition cars. The Italians were the leading proponents of such bravura motor sports. Races like the Mille Miglia and the Targa Florio pitted Europe's leading drivers and racing machines against a grueling schedule and generally horrible roads. Only the French have kept something of

this tradition alive with the Paris-Dakkar Rally. In its early years, the twenty-four hours of LeMans was also a road race, but its enduring popularity and increasing importance brought it mostly off the country roads and onto a regulated, closed circuit.

The Carrera Panamericana was conceived to celebrate and publicize the completion of the Pan-American Highway, which ran the entire length of Mexico, from Texas in the north to Guatemala in the south, linking the United States with Central America. With historic participation by Porsche, Lancia, Ferrari, Mercedes-Benz, and other European marques, the Carrera

By the fifth Carrera in 1954, tech inspections had become harder, and few modifications were allowed in the sedan class. The Lincoln team was known for stretching the rules but not breaking them. *Credit: Henry Ford Museum and Greenfield Village; Photographer: Mackenzie*

became one of the most celebrated motoring events of the 1950s. It was also a career builder for a number of world-class drivers. When the first Carrera Panamericana was announced, it was greeted with skepticism. Racers had visions of gasoline that was half diesel oil and banditos hiding behind every rock. But a cash prize from the Mexican government and the eventual support of the American Automobile Association (AAA) gave the venture credibility and signaled a rush among international competitors to get onto the starting grid.

While it lasted, the Carrera was a car-busting challenge that tested men and machines to the limit through six days of flat-out racing over a number of marked stages totaling 2,136 miles. No other race in history saw the immortal Mercedes-Benz 300SL wearing windshield guards, known as "buzzard bars." Unfortunately, due to the lax enforcement of the race route by the federales, the race suffered a number of fatalities both among competitors and spectators and was canceled after 1954, its fifth tumultuous year, never to be run again.

In the late 1940s and early 1950s, Lincoln made a major course correction and changed its image in a burn-the-bridges manner that targeted Buick and Oldsmobile as competitors rather than Packard or Cadillac. Lincoln now had a powerful new ohv V-8 on its hands and cars that drove very well, thanks to chief engineer Earle MacPherson's industry-leading front ball-joint suspension. One way to get people talking about Lincoln would be to claim a motor sports victory, but it couldn't be just any race.

As in the days of Henry Ford himself, racing was a powerful way to build a reputation overnight. Mercury had been involved in racing as a regular thing, especially at Daytona Beach. The winged-foot cars were in on the beginnings of stock car racing in the South. But Lincoln, with its prestigious image, had always been too far above the greasy fingernail world of racing.

Bob Estes, an influential Lincoln dealer in California, supported the Carrera Panamericana. When it looked as though Americans might ignore the race due to fears about the quality of Mexican gasoline and the fickleness of the federales, he went down to Mexico and drove the race route himself. When he returned, he placed ads in the newspapers saying that the Carrera was feasible and should happen. He was also influential in assembling the Lincoln team that would cover itself with glory in the years ahead.

In 1950, the first year of the Panamericana, Bill Stroppe, the legendary desert racer, and his partner, driver Johnny Mantz, entered a near-stock Lincoln in the sedan class. Stroppe's excellent preparation for the race and the strength of Lincoln's 336.7ci V-8 engine (at 152bhp) put them at the front of the pack after several days. Stroppe and Mantz ran flat out day after day, alternating the lead several times against Ray Elliot and NASCAR racing legend Hershel McGriff, in an Oldsmobile.

In the end, Stroppe and Mantz were beaten by fate. Although none of the racers knew it until they got there, the last 107 miles of their race route, the stretch from Tuxtla Gutierrez to El Ocotal, were still unpaved—it was raw dirt road! Although Johnny Mantz had an advanced case of Montezuma's Revenge and was feeling terrible, he still drove the Lincoln at race-winning speeds, until they reached that last section of road. Then the fast pace of the race simply demolished their tires. McGriff and Elliot combed the little town of Tuxtla Gutierrez and found some General tires of the right size for their Olds. These tires had beefy six-ply sidewalls, in contrast to the two-ply tires on Stroppe's car. The Generals were almost indestructible on the broken, rock-strewn dirt road that concluded the race. The Lincoln of Stroppe and Mantz ran like a gazelle, but it burst its tires well before the finish line. They even drove on one bare rim to finish, but the victory went to Oldsmobile, McGriff, and Elliot. While a win would have been better, the second-place finish of the Lincoln came as a surprise to many, even at the Lincoln-Mercury Division.

Despite a few unpleasant encounters, the Carrera Panamericana had been a clear success. It proved to be a stirring road race; it brought vital tourism to Mexico, and it gave the new Lincolns a much-needed shot of publicity. When the Mexican government announced that there would be another Carrera the following year, with a few revisions, the international racing community came on board in a big way.

The 1951 race saw some major changes—one might say improvements. First, the Mexican automobile club, the Asociacion Nacional Automoviles, became the official organizer of the race, taking the Mexican government out of the loop. The rules still allowed for stock cars, but now it was possible to modify the engines for better breathing. Second, and most important, the race route was turned upside down. The race would begin at the southern tip of Mexico and end in Ciudad Juarez on the Texas border, to give press and public easier access to the finish. While there were fewer starters in 1951 than in 1950 (ninety-one versus 132), the second running of the Carrera was a more sophisticated and professional race than before.

The 1951 Carrera was a triumph for the Europeans. Piero Taruffi won it in a Ferrari, and his teammate Alberto Ascari took second. William Sterling finished third in a Chrysler; Troy Ruttman and Clay Smith placed fourth in a hot-rod '48 Mercury.

The Lincoln team set its sights on the 1952 race, and they were there in force. Engine tuner Clay Smith and Bill Stroppe headed the Lincoln effort for 1952.

Winning was one thing the Panamericana Lincolns did quite well, thank you. After the first year of the race, the route was reversed so that the enduro ended in Oaxaca, closer to the US border. In 1952, '53, and '54, Lincolns won the sedan class of the race, thanks to careful preparation and fast, solid vehicles. *Credit: Henry Ford Museum and Greenfield Village; Photographer: Mackenzie*

They were well prepared but would need every bit of luck and skill they had to match competitors from Porsche, Ferrari, Mercedes-Benz, and others. Fortunately, the organizers had instituted two classes, the stock car division and a sports car class, so that the Lincolns and Ferraris were not racing directly against each other.

Stroppe, who had been a hot-rodder and desert racer, put his experience to good use. He and Clay Smith worked up a modification schedule for the Lincolns that would give them more power and better handling. These tweaks included using early production 1953 model-year cars for the race, installing high-lift cams and solid lifters (from a Ford truck engine), porting the intake manifolds for better breathing, and installing dual exhausts, which the factory cunningly listed as an option at the last minute.

These 1953 Lincolns raced with the GM Hydra-Matic three-speed automatic transmissions that all Lincolns used. These units were unmodified but blueprinted, that is, brought up to exact specifications internally. Brakes were improved with a heavy-duty lining, and most of the Lincoln racers used two small 12-volt fans in the trunk to clear fumes from the driver's area and to cool the rear brakes. Stock springs and

Could we make it any clearer for you? This operations board at the final Carrera in 1954 shows the detail to which the Lincoln team, headed by Bill Stroppe, used to organize their participation. Everything about the cars, the pit stops, and personnel is on this board. Just get in your car and race, OK? *Credit: Henry Ford Museum and Greenfield Village; Photographer: Mackenzie*

shocks were replaced with the stiffer "export" springs, and the multiple shocks were powerful units from Gabriel and Houdaille.

Everything unnecessary was stripped from the race cars, including radios and back seats. That created a little extra room for auxiliary fuel tanks, bringing total capacity per car to 41 gallons. Stroppe and Smith also sent dozens of Firestone racing tires to Mexico—inflated with inert nitrogen gas for better temperature stability in the scorching deserts. Stroppe's desert racing experience was a winning card for the Lincoln team. He combined experience with a genius for details. Stroppe himself went down to Mexico to prerun the course.

He recalls: "Then we came back and started all over again and did things that we were getting lined up for

race day. Every race we would try to do better, try to find something that would give us a quick start, or even up. Got down to the point where we went to bed early and did whatever we could to make sure that everything went off right."

"We tried several ways of running it. One particular leg, we changed the tires before we made that leg, and that gave us pretty good tires that wouldn't blow, you know? In other words, the right tire is king for high speeds. Clay Smith was my partner and, of course, I rode with Johnny Mantz. Clay rode with Chuck Stevensen, and we were very, very close to each other."

"At night we would meet the other Lincoln teams after we went as far as you could go in the daylight and trade tips. We'd say, 'Come on, out with it, let us know!'

Ready to go again, this mid-1950s Lincoln is about to undergo tech inspection for the La Carrera in 1989. The La Carrera is a recreation of the famous Carrera Panamericana, but it is run from Ensenada on the west coast of Baja California to San Felipe on the east coast of Baja. The course includes twisting mountain roads and a final blast across a scorching desert. *Credit: G. Von Dare*

And then I made Johnny Mantz go to bed. Just as soon as he got in at night, I told him, 'I don't want you talking to anybody; go to bed.' And it worked."

"I had a jack with a big heavy strap on it, so that if we got upside-down it wouldn't start bouncing off us! I saw a lot of guys have trouble by not thinking a little bit before the race started."

The winning potential of the Lincoln team drew heavy interest from the factory. Stroppe said that, ". . . Benson Ford (then head of the L-M Division) was there. All of 'em tried to follow us as much as they could, and then they just said the hell with it, we're gonna fly from one point to the other. I felt pretty bad about Ben. He was a very white label person. And he was so doggoned careful; he didn't want to put us out of business with the rules. So I'd say, 'Ben, go down to the gas station and get us another gallon of oil,' or something like that. He'd never done anything like

that, he'd never got his hands dirty before."

Overall, it was a large task force that Lincoln put in the field for the '52 race. According to Stroppe, "We had a big truck with a lot of spare parts in it that got to the place about three o'clock in the morning. There was a lot of stuff that we went through, especially brake shoes, stuff like that. We had the shoes already made for each wheel, and we tested them too. I had one man that did nothing but the brake drums. And I wouldn't let anybody else touch the brake drums, even me."

All that preparation paid off handsomely, with Lincolns finishing one, two, and three in the sedan division, and a nonfactory Lincoln driven by Ray Crawford placing fourth. The people in Dearborn were thrilled.

In 1953, the Carrera was again run in November, but the rules and tech inspections became harder. Some of the modifications permitted in 1952 were outlawed,

Was the Carrera a tough race? Ask this Lincoln prerunner used to test the course. Any small misstep or loss of concentration over the six-day length of the Carrera, and you went home in a basket. *Credit: Henry Ford Museum and Greenfield Village; Photographer: Mackenzie*

and the Lincoln team had to rely on mostly stock engines and chassis, with some modifications for carrying extra fuel and bigger brakes. Cosmopolitan Sport Coupes were the vehicles of choice. Another, much tougher rule for '53 was that all vehicles would be impounded three hours after the finish of each leg, making extensive repairs impossible and putting a premium on the strength of the basic car itself. For 1953, Lincoln shone. Not only did Lincolns claim the top four places at the finish, but a group of privately entered cars did almost as well as the factory team, finishing eighth, ninth, and tenth.

Call it the peak; 1953 was a banner year for Lincoln's performance image, and the division responded with an ad campaign that placed a road race Lincoln in the background while a young couple enjoyed a production car in the foreground. It was also the last year that the brilliant Clay Smith would be a part of Lincoln's race efforts. He was killed in September 1954 at a dirt track race in Illinois, leaving a forlorn Bill Stroppe to manage the next event alone.

The 1954 Carrera was all drama for Lincoln. A look at the entry list shows a total of fifteen factory and private Lincolns entered in the race. But this year, the toll was heavy. Five Lincolns were eliminated on the first day, and many of the others were not competitive. During the

second day of competition, Bill Voukovitch crashed out the final factory car. This left only the private entry of Ray Crawford with a hope for the win. And worst of all, a Cadillac driven by Keith Andrew looked like it just might take the prize that year. The Cadillac actually ran better on the two fastest legs of the race.

But Crawford was no easy target. He ran the tires off his Lincoln and finished a scant three minutes ahead of the Caddy. Lincoln had won again, even if it was not with the steamroller ease of years past. Lincoln basked in the worldwide recognition that it had a superior product.

Unfortunately, a trend was developing worldwide that was bad news for road-based motor sports. All races run on public roads (the Mille Miglia, Targa Florio, and Tour de France) were in jeopardy as speeds increased and populations grew, defeating the organizers' ability to control crowds, as well as entrants.

In the case of the Carrera Panamericana, it was only a matter of time. The Mexican government had fulfilled its purpose early on when the first two races called worldwide attention to Mexico and its newly constructed roads. Mexico was not interested in furthering the careers of road racers and car manufacturers, no matter how much glamour they brought to the proceedings. And the several fatalities of rural people and competitors made it much harder for the government to ignore the reality of a race that tied up a whole country for a week. So, by 1955, the Carrera was history.

Despite the strangeness of this enterprise, the buzzard bars, the unfinished roads, the burros around the next blind bend, the legacy of the Mexican road race lives on in the name of Porsche's most advanced model, the Carrera, and in the long memories of Lincoln owners who briefly tasted the sweet nectar of victory, mixed with the flavorful bouquet of sangria. Few Lincoln owners in the 1990s realize that their luxurious cars were once a force to be reckoned with in the world of motor sports.

As an interesting side note, a re-creation of the Mexican road race called the "La Carrera," is being run in the 1990s. Amazingly enough, some of the Lincolns that competed in the original outings still gather in Baja California to rev their engines on a foggy morning and set off for a day of high-speed racing. As in the old days, the Porsches and Ferraris may win the overall crown, but those elegant, all-American hot-rod Lincolns still come across the finish line with a flash of old glory and some serious speed.

Index